# Ancient Greek Civilization
## Part I

# Professor Jeremy McInerney

THE TEACHING COMPANY ®

PUBLISHED BY:

THE TEACHING COMPANY
4151 Lafayette Center Drive, Suite 100
Chantilly, Virginia 20151-1232
1-800-TEACH-12
Fax—703-378-3819
www.teach12.com

ISBN 1-56585-809-3

# Jeremy McInerney, Ph.D.

Associate Professor
Department of Classical Studies,University of Pennsylvania

Jeremy McInerney received his Ph.D. from the University of California, Berkeley, in 1992. He was the Wheeler Fellow at the American School of Classical Studies at Athens, and has excavated in Israel, at Corinth and on Crete. Since 1992 has been teaching Greek History at the University of Pennsylvania, where he held the Laura Jan Meyerson Term Chair in the Humanities from 1994 to 1998. He is currently an associate professor in the Department of Classical Studies and Chair of the Graduate Group in the Art and Archaeology of the Mediterranean World. Professor McInerney also serves on the Managing Committee of the American School of Classical Studies at Athens.

Professor McInerney's research interests include topography, epigraphy, and historiography. He has published articles in the *American Journal of Archaeology*, *Hesperia*, and *California Studies in Classical Antiquity*. In 1997 he was an invited participant at a colloquium on ethnicity in the ancient world, hosted by the Center for Hellenic Studies in Washington. His book, *The Folds of Parnassos: Land and Ethnicity in Ancient Phokis*, is a study of state formation and ethnic identity in the Archaic and Classical periods, and it will be published by the University of Texas Press in 1999.

# Table of Contents

## Ancient Greek Civilization
## Part I

# Ancient Greek Civilization

**Scope:**

The Greeks enjoy a special place in the construction of western culture and identity. Much of what we esteem in our own culture derives from them: democracy, epic poetry, lyric poetry, tragedy, history writing, philosophy, aesthetic taste, all of these and many other features of cultural life enter the West from Greece. The oracle of Apollo at Delphi had inscribed over the temple, "Know Thyself." For us, that also means knowing the Greeks.

In these lectures we will cover the period from the late Bronze Age, c. 1500 B.C., down to the time of Philip of Macedon and Alexander the Great, in the late fourth century B.C., concentrating on the two hundred year interval from 600 to 400 B.C. The lectures will proceed chronologically and draw on the rich literary and archaeological sources of Greek history, from Homer's majestic *Odyssey* to Schliemann's excavations and Troy and Mycenae, from Aeschylus' *Oresteia* to the wealthy Greek colonies of Sicily. Lectures introduce the audience to the world of classical Athens, described in the histories of Herodotus and Thucydides and the dialogues of Plato.

The lectures explore the similarities and differences between Greek culture and our own. In a variety of areas, such as in religion and gender, the Greeks seem alien, approaching the world in ways utterly different from our ways. In other facets of social life, on the other hand, such as in politics and war, we find a culture perhaps not very unlike our own. We will examine each of these aspects of Greek culture in an attempt to understand better how Greek culture developed as it did, and why it still resonates for us today.

# Lecture One
# Greece and the Western World

**Scope:**

This lecture introduces the audience to the role and importance of the Greeks in the formation of Western culture. We will look at the rediscovery of Greek culture in the modern period and discuss how identifying with a classical culture often means ignoring real differences between the Greeks and ourselves. We state the theme of the course, which is to examine both the similarities and differences between ourselves and the Greeks, in order to understand how their culture was formed and how we are connected to it.

# Outline

**I.** Introduction.

    **A.** In a host of different ways—in the areas of democracy, poetry, theater, history writing, philosophy, aesthetic taste, and architecture and sculpture—the cultural life of the West derives from Greek models. A good example of this connection is Freud's use of the Oedipus myth to explain a central feature of psychoanalytic theory: the Oedipus complex.

    **B.** Nevertheless, there are crucial differences between the ancient Greeks and modern Western society, differences that have often been glossed over because of the deep attachment we feel to Greek culture. Two areas illustrate the complex relationship between the modern and ancient worlds: democracy and theater.

        **1.** Unlike modern *representative* democracy, ancient Athenian democracy involved the direct participation of every adult male citizen.

        **2.** Although modern theater finds its antecedents in Greek drama, the two also had important differences.

            **a.** Only a few dramatic performances were given in ancient Greece each year.

            **b.** Greek drama was performed in the setting of a religious festival in honor of the god Dionysus.

        **3.** Our versions of both of these institutions are different in important ways from their Greek models.

**C.** The theme of the course, then, is to explore the complex relationship between the Greeks and ourselves. What made the culture of ancient Greece one to which we feel such affinity? In what ways was it also really quite different from our own?

**II.** The Rediscovery of the Greeks.

**A.** Even in the Renaissance, classical culture was primarily equated with Roman culture and Latin literature. The rediscovery of the Greeks was the product of German historian and art critic Johannes Winkelmann and the "philhellenic movement" of the 18$^{th}$ and 19$^{th}$ centuries.

**B.** Early travellers such as Dodwell and Leake also helped create the Romantic image of an ideal, perfect, classical Greece by describing and drawing its architectural ruins.

**C.** Since then, Greek culture has helped to define, for better or for worse, a Western canon: a body of thought and art that somehow defines the West.

    **1.** Many have sought to retrieve this ideal image of a beautiful Greece by studying and trying to imitate the ancient Greeks and their culture.

    **2.** Following the battle of Jena, the Prussian minister of education announced that he would reconstruct Prussian society on the ancient Greek model. There was a tendency in German thought to seek perfection by returning to the Greeks.

    **3.** In many respects, the Greeks are the idealized version of what we seek to become. However, they were just as human and imperfect as we are.

**III.** *Alterité* and Greece as a Forerunner of Western Culture.

**A.** During the last two centuries Western countries, including the United States, have developed national identities through a dual process: seeing themselves as the cultural descendants of the classical Greeks, and as the opposites of other societies, especially those of the East, which are regarded as different and opposite.

    **1.** All too often, classical studies have been put to the service of helping a given society justify its own sense of cultural superiority over other societies.

**2.** This tendency is evident in our own architecture, poetry, drama, political life, and even popular entertainment. The television sitcom, for instance, has its roots in the "new comedy" of the Greek playwright Menander.

**B.** To break this temptation to venerate the Greeks as enlightened demigods, we should try to understand them on their own terms. Their accomplishments remain impressive, and our connections to them remain fundamental, but we may better understand both their culture and our own if we study the Greeks as they actually were rather than as we would like them to have been.

## Suggested Reading

Marchand, S.L. (1996) *Down from Olympus. Archaeology and Philhellenism in Germany, 1750-1970.* Princeton: Princeton University Press.

Cartledge, P. (1993) *The Greeks. A Portrait of Self and Others.* Oxford: Opus Books. ch. 1.

## Questions to Consider

1. What do we mean by the term "classical"?

2. In what sense are we indebted to the Greeks?

3. Is it possible to study Greek culture dispassionately, or must we always suffer under what one historian has called "the dead hand of the Past"?

# Lecture One—Transcript
# Greece and the Western World

Welcome to this, our series of lectures on Ancient Greek Civilization. My name is Jeremy McInerney and in the course of the next twenty four lectures, what I would like to do is introduce you to the world of Greek culture and the accomplishments of the Greeks. Today, to begin, I'd like to talk a little bit about what it was that the Greeks produced and how we as a culture much later relate to the accomplishment of the Greeks.

In order to clarify this right from the start and to give you an idea of what it is that I want to do in both this lecture and the rest of this series, I'd like to start with a story of an episode that occurred a few years ago, when I was an undergraduate. I sat in a lecture where the lecturer talking about Greek religion began by saying, "It's very important when we study the Greeks to pay close attention to their religion and their thought system." I was sitting in the audience thinking, "This is very good. He's showing proper respect for them."

He then proceeded to tell a series of stories about how when the Greeks worshiped their gods, they performed sacrifices where they cut animals open and played with their livers and intestines to try to divine what was happening in the future. As he was telling these various stories, he was grimacing and leering, and trying to elicit a reaction from the undergraduates. He was quite successful in making them think that the Greeks were somehow very odd, weird, and inferior to us and to our conception of how to deal with God.

What the episode crystallized for me was that we have a real difficulty when we approach the Greeks because we have a tendency either to think of the Greeks as being demi-gods—a culture that accomplished more than we could ever hope to and a culture in whose shadow we live—or else as somehow being so alien and different than we can never really understand them at all. In some sense, it's those two poles that I want to navigate in the course of these lectures to try to think about the ways in which we are alike to the Greeks and the ways in which we are very different from the Greeks. I don't want to turn them into gods and I don't want to turn them into comic book characters either. Rather, I want to think about them as a culture that was extremely important for us.

There's no doubt that it is a culture which is in a way a bedrock of Western civilization. Some people like to advance the argument that we should study the Greeks because they are more important to us than any other culture and that their culture is unique. That's a claim that you might want to think about. In what sense is any culture unique or better than others? All cultures are unique, I would argue. Japanese culture, Chinese culture, Indian culture—we even know now that cultures that were once dismissed as "primitive" in fact have extremely rich cultural lives. The epistemology and the cosmology of the aborigines or of the plains Indians—these are extremely interesting and exciting.

Nevertheless, whether it's a historical accident or not, the case remains that we are somehow closely tied to the Greeks, for better off or worse, if you will. Think of it, for example, in these terms: when Freud late in the 19th and early in the 20th century worked on the human subconscious, he tried to find a term to explain a particular complex which he had isolated whereby young boys feel an urge to kill their fathers and to take their place, ideally in a marriage with their mother, a stage through which he says we hopefully move beyond into a more mature adult phase psychologically. He used as a label to give expression to that complex the "Oedipus complex," using a Greek myth to give it a name. Why? Because we go back to the Greeks. We somehow see them as being earlier than us and a bedrock that we can rely on—a culture that we're related to.

There are two other ways in which I think we can look at the Greeks and think about their relationship to us. For example, we often point out that we live in a democracy. Democracy is a term coined from two Greek words: *demos* and *kratia*—the "rule of the people." Are we like the Greeks in the sense that we are democratic? We'll explore that in a moment.

Another area in which we show a kind of descent from the Greeks, in which they are our ancestors, is in the world of theater. Again, "theater" is originally a Greek word. If you go to a theater in the round looking down at a stage where there may be an orchestra beneath the stage, you are looking at an architectural form that the Greeks devised and which was then carried on by the Romans and later taken up by Western European civilization. In both these respects, we seem to be intimately connected to the Greeks. To understand them would be to understand ourselves a little bit better.

On the other hand, to look at that other pole—we're like them but we're also different from them—consider some of these aspects of the two things I've just talked about. In relation to democracy, for example, our notion of democracy is that we elect representatives who serve on our behalf. The Greeks wouldn't have understood that as a democratic principle at all. For them, democracy was participatory. You and I are the *demos* and the power of the people means that we deliberate make the final decisions about what our state will do. Peace treaties, the treatment of ambassadors, whether we stay or go, whether we abandon Athens in the face of the Persian onslaught: these are decisions that we the people make, not our elected representatives. Even though we call ourselves a democracy, our conception of democracy—of electoral districts, of representatives, of congressmen—these are all things that the Greeks would not have ever understood.

In our democracy, we rely on political parties, the Democrats and the Republicans in this country. The notion of the political party is something that the Greeks would not have understood. Instead, individual men (and I'm afraid here we have to acknowledge that there is no role for women in Greek democracy, another slight difference between theirs and ours) have friends and associates—cliques or factions, if you will. That's the nearest that the Greeks get to political parties. In that respect, too, their democracy is very different from our own. We can compare our democracy to one in which every adult male citizen who had served his military service is able to stand up and to speak in front of the people.

What about theater? It would seem, since the architecture of theaters is much the same now as it was then, that the idea of a performance and an audience really can't have changed a great deal. After all, you can still go to Epidaurus in Greece and see a performance of a Greek play, so surely we're still connected to the Greeks in that respect.

Yes and no. Yes, we are, in the sense that we still perform their plays. We're still excited by the majesty of the poetry of people like Sophocles, Euripides and Aeschylus, but in another respect ancient theater and modern theater are completely different.

Consider these factors, for example: you can go to the theater if you live in New York any night of the week. If you decide to go to the theater, you can choose any one of 50 plays on Broadway or off. In Athens, theatrical performances are limited to only a couple of days each year. Much more significantly, those days in the Athenian calendar when you can go to see a dramatic performance are religious festivals. When you go to church or synagogue or when you go to the theater, you're going to two very different things, I'd maintain in our culture. But if you're a Greek and you're going to a theatrical performance, the first thing you'll see will be a sacrifice performed on the altar by the priests who are presiding over that religious festival. That entire performance will be conducted to the greater glory and in honor of a god, usually Dionysus.

There is a god watching over the performance and the performance takes place during his festival. It isn't something where you can choose a play here or a play there. There is one set of plays on one day of the festival, another set of plays on the next day of the festival, and another set of plays on the next day of the festival. The entire community—not just people who are lucky to buy tickets that Saturday night—is present at this religious theatrical festival.

In just these two areas where it's so easy to think that we are the descendents of the Greeks, we see illustrated this idea that for as much as we are like the Greeks, we are also in many respects quite different from them. That makes it very difficult in some respects to understand their world clearly.

In order to understand how we relate to the Greeks, we have to begin this series of lectures by talking a little bit about how the discipline of classical studies and ancient history came about. How is it that if you go to a university, there will be a college professor trained to teach you this particular material? How do we frame the Greeks? How do we turn them into something that we can teach?

Classical culture is not something that we've remained connected to throughout the centuries going back to the ancient world at all. In fact, as you probably all know, after the Middle Ages, in the Renaissance (the very name of the period means the "rebirth") there was a rediscovery of much of ancient culture. Yet, most of the ancient culture that was rediscovered during that period was actually Roman and Latin—the culture of Rome and Italy and the culture of the Latin language.

The Greeks really lagged behind, partly because most people couldn't read Greek and partly because many of the texts had not yet been discovered and opened up for study. You remember the famous adage about Shakespeare, a man who knew little Latin and less Greek.

For a long time, Western Europe was aware of the fact that there had been a Greek culture, but they were not terribly clear on what that culture had really been like because they knew of it mainly through a Latin filter—through the filter of Roman culture. The rediscovery of the Greeks really begins to take off in the 18th and 19th centuries. It's especially associated with German scholars and in particular a German art historian and critic, Johann Winkelmann.

Not only did he show that there were Greek vases in Italy that attested to a much earlier, more wonderful culture—an aesthetically advanced culture—but at the same time, the same period saw the development of a movement known as the "philhellenic movement." It means quite literally the "lovers of the Greeks." There is quite a specific political value to that term, because as you probably know, up until the early 19th century, Greece was actually under the control of the Turkish Empire. The power of Turkey, looming on the edges of Greece, was something that the Western powers were concerned about. It seemed as if the support of Greek culture was in a way a kind of claim to make Greece European and to save it from the Turk.

At the same time, many Greeks themselves were beginning to agitate for independence. There was a very bloodthirsty war of independence fought in Greece in the 1820s, from which we can date the origins of the modern Greek nation. The support that Western countries gave to Greece at that time was very much predicated on the notion that they were saving Greece because Greece was the culture that was the core root culture from which Western European culture came.

You find a curious combination of both scholarship and contemporary politics in the works of some of the most influential writers of the period in the 19th century. I'm referring to travel writers. These are usually only studied now by specialists, but they make great reading and I strongly recommend you go back and look at the works of some of these men like Dodwell, William Leake, the German Ross, and the Frenchman de Tocqueville.

These men who traveled to Greece in the early part of the 19th century were going largely into an unknown land. They took with them as their guide the ancient travel writer Pausanias and what they did, quite simply, was to walk or ride on horseback around Greece and say, "Pausanias says that in his time there was a temple at this location and when I went there, I could still see these pillars or these walls."

What you have is a flood of material being printed in England, Germany and France in the early part of the 19th century in which these scouts and writers (they are actually sometimes military spies who are looking at the Greek countryside in case their armies were ever going to have to come south) are looking at Greece and they're seeing it both as a modern country that may have to be saved from the Turk and as an ancient culture to which they are intimately tied.

We find a combination, then, of classical Greece and the contemporary world in the 19th century being drawn together. We see this reflected in the art of the period as well. Artists flocking to Greece begin to produce these wonderful drawings of the ruins to be seen in the Greek countryside—these very romantic visions of the Greek world.

This romantic vision of a lost Greece is an interesting one because it turns Greece almost into a kind of Eden, a land from which we came and which we may be able to get back to if we read enough about the Greeks and resuscitate their culture. It led to the idea, for example, that ancient Greece must have been a soft and verdant countryside, almost like Kent or the Home Counties outside of London. When people went to Greece in the 19th century and actually saw how spare, rough, dry and Spartan most of the landscape is, people were concerned about this. They believed that the ancient countryside must have been debased over the centuries as people plowed too much and overused the land and that now Greece is only a watered-down, debased version of what it once was.

That's not actually true. Ecological studies in this century have demonstrated that the Greek countryside of the Classical Age was pretty much the same as the Greek countryside of today. The most significant changes in Greece have probably been in the post-war period since deep-bore irrigation was introduced.

Leaving that aside, the point I'm making here is that what we see in the 19th century, for all these various reasons, is the creation of an idea—of an ideal Greece, a Greece that is beautiful and gone, but may be one that we can get back to if we study the Greeks and particularly if we model ourselves on the Greeks.

Throughout much of the 19th century, the focus for this was in German scholarship, but it wasn't just scholarship. It was in German life, particularly in Prussia. After the defeat of the Prussians at the Battle of Jena by Napoleon, the Prussian Minister for Education issued a manifesto, which claimed that he was going to rebuild Prussian society along the model of the ancient Greeks. Throughout the 18th and 19th centuries, you find in many parts of German culture—in the works of many German poets and thinkers, in Schiller, and in Holderlin—time and time again the notion expressed that while we modern Europeans live in a fractured world and an imperfect world, we could perfect it. We could reclaim perfection if we were to get back to the world of the Greeks. That was somehow the Eden from which we've all descended.

The Greeks have had to carry a very heavy weight on their backs. They have been for the last 200 years the model not just of what we are, but the idealized version of what we might be—that if we didn't have to put up with unfortunate scandals such as either Watergate or more recently Monicagate, then we could expect a political life in which our statesmen were truly statesmen-like. No culture should have to carry the weight of those expectations. The Greeks were every bit as human as we are.

In the course of these lectures, we're going to look at various aspects of Greek culture and life and try to get away from this very freighted view of the Greeks as "us perfected." What I will be doing, then, in the course of the lectures is trying to give us a clearer conception of what the Greeks accomplished.

There's finally one last aspect of the modern treatment of the Greeks that we need to address, and it's this: over the course of about the last two centuries, as the modern nation states of England, Germany, France and the United States have taken shape and moved out of being earlier kingdoms or constituting themselves as republics, they've developed national identities. All nations have this at some point. National identities are created out of a dual process. They're created out of a consideration of what we once were—of our past—

and of what the other cultures and civilizations are around us, the ones that we deal with. This is a process often referred to with the fancy term of "alterité." We look at another culture or civilization and we see in it the opposite of ourselves. We take our values and we abstract the negative on to the other.

In the course of this century, we have certainly seen that in the way that we in the Western world have looked at the Soviet Union as it once was. Now that the Soviet Union is gone, we have much different feelings about the Russians. We thought of that world as being in some sense diametrically our opposite.

More generally speaking, over the last 200 years in the West, there has been a strong notion that we all in the West—and that means Western Europe, the English-speaking world and North America—are somehow different from the East. This has been a product of our colonial experience and history. It has meant that we have had to think of ourselves somehow as being culturally quite distinct.

Part of that process of identifying what we are as opposed to what they are has been to think about our past and what we've come from. The whole enterprise of studying the ancient world has really often been tainted by this notion of finding some kind of cultural superiority in the West—a superiority of our way of doing things. Whereas the East could point to Confucian philosophy and the aesthetic accomplishments of the Chinese or the Japanese, the Western version of this has been to go back to our Classical roots.

If, for example, you walk down a place like the mall in Washington, you will see buildings, all of which carry a particular message. They are neo-classical in their design. Why? Because the classical world is the world that defines what we regard as being culturally superior and desirable.

If you go to the Second National Bank in Philadelphia, one of the most wonderful early buildings of the 19th century, you'll see a building which is virtually a Doric temple. As you walk past that, you can look at the architecture of it and think about the quality of the stone and design, but what you really should be thinking is what does it say about us that we chose to use that design—that temple—to stand for our banking system, as opposed to using, say, a Japanese temple? It's equally interesting architecturally, but somehow one that doesn't evoke in us a sense of continuity or stability.

Look at our poetry: one of the Nobel Prize winners of recent years was Derek Walcott's 'Omerus' (which in Greek is "Homer")—epic poetry again still showing its vitality. Whether it be in our drama and the plays we go to; whether it be in our architecture; whether it be in our politics—in whatever area we look at, we tie ourselves to the Greeks consciously or unconsciously, sometimes being very close to Greek culture and sometimes being a little bit further away from the original model.

Let me then turn to one final example that moves away from the high world of the Parthenon and the Second National Bank, or from politics and theater, to something more in our daily lives. I think even there we can demonstrate this kind of strange connection that we have to the Greeks. One of the most questionable gifts of American culture to the world in the last 30 years has been the sitcom: on TV, 30 minutes dedicated to looking at the travails of a particular family.

Usually the whole setting of the show is indoors: it's in the family room, whether it be "Father Knows Best" back in the 1950s through to ones in the 1980s. The whole focus of this drama will be one particular family, the relations in that family and the trials and tribulations of those individuals. The world that it creates is nearly always apolitical. It does not refer to the wider political world going on. Rather, it reduces the world simply to the dilemmas of individual men and women.

The background or genre from which that comes, you may be surprised to know, is in fact a Greek genre that goes back to the fourth century B.C. It is in that time (we may have time at the end of these lectures to get as far as this) at the end of the fourth century B.C. that Menander, the Greek poet, produced a series of comedies known collectively as "new comedy." They were very different from the old world of Aristophanes, where the plays had been about politics, the plays had been obscene, and where the characters had worn large phalluses and had looked ridiculous on stage. Characters like Cleon, who really could have been the ancient Bill Clinton in the way he's treated in these plays, are treated as buffoons. They're put on the stage and ridiculed by the community.

New comedy was very different. By the end of the classical period, the Greeks had moved away from that politically engaged comedy and instead had turned to a type of comedy in which the entire focus was just the family. There was no greater political world, no community, no *demos*, no Athens—just Mum, Dad, the girl and her boyfriend who she wants to marry but who the family won't allow her to marry because he's not of the right status, and the very happy and intelligent slave who manages to save everybody's life in the end.

It's very interesting to stop and think about what sort of change took place in the Greek world between the fifth century B.C. and the fourth century B.C. I raise this to make one final point. We have a tendency when we think about the Greeks to think in monolithic terms, that is, to think of Greek culture as being a single, homogenous culture. Usually it's associated with the age of Pericles, so that you can think of one great statesman, one great city (Athens), one great culture producing Sophocles, Euripides and earlier than that Aeschylus, and one culture producing Plato and Socrates.

But in fact, the world of the Greeks is vastly more complex than that. During the next 24 lectures, I want to take you on a survey of all of Greek culture, from the Bronze Age going back as early as about 3000 B.C. and taking us right forward to the end of the Bronze Age around 1100 B.C. Then taking us down through the Geometric, the Archaic, and the Classical periods (the Classical period being our focus in the second half of the course of lectures), where we'll deal with the fifth and fourth centuries B.C. Unfortunately, we can't take our survey much further than that, although there is of course plenty of Greek history that follows after.

What we'll find over the course of these lectures is that, particularly from the period of about 1600 B.C. to about 300 B.C., we're going to see a culture undergoing astonishing changes. The Bronze Age will be very different from the Iron Age. The Iron Age will itself undergo many changes. What we're going to find is the record of accomplishment of a civilization which produced much that is lasting in Western culture, but much that we have to examine closely.

We talked about the Parthenon earlier and I'm going to finish with the Parthenon. We'll come back to it later in the lectures, but I want you to consider this. It is a perfection of Greek architecture without doubt. It has cunning techniques of tricking the eye so that columns that are bent look straight. It is a masterpiece that we have copied over and over again in different forms. But in the context of its own times, what is the Parthenon? It is a building that was paid for by the tribute that Athens received from the allied states around the Aegean. Originally, they were its allies in a war against the Persians, but by the middle of the fifth century B.C., they are the subjects of the Athenian mistress—the Athenian empire.

What we're going to find is that much that seems familiar to us in this series of lectures, when put in the context of its own time, will assume a very different look. A building, which may be gorgeous to look at, can actually carry with it a great deal more meaning—a hidden meaning that we'll try to discover in the course of the next 24 lectures.

# Lecture Two
# Minoan Crete

**Scope:**

The second millenium B.C. witnessed two extraordinary civilizations in Greece: Minoan Crete and the Mycenaean culture of the mainland. In this lecture we examine the first of these two, the civilization of Bronze Age Crete. The distinctive nature of Minoan sites at Knossos, Mallia, Phaistos and Zakro has led archaeologists to dub this culture a palatial society, in which the magnificent Minoan palaces served as the administrative, religious, and economic centers of a society that was highly complex and hierarchically structured.

The fact that this society has left no literature and is known entirely through the work of archaeologists poses questions for us. To what extent can archaeology alone recreate the story of a culture? Minoan Crete also demonstrates the degree to which we remain indebted to the work of 19th-century archaeologists like Sir Arthur Evans, amateurs in the true sense of the word.

# Outline

I. Before the Greeks. As in other parts of the world, a succession of societies of increasing complexity has left traces across Greece.

    **A.** At the Franchthi Cave, excavations reveal a society of hunter-gatherers in contact with the islands.

    **B.** Sesklo and Dimini, Neolithic settlements in central Greece, display complex social organization in the fifth and fourth millennia B.C.

    **C.** Cycladic culture, located in the Greek islands, has left evidence of specialized trade and manufacturing in the form of exquisite marble figurines. We know very little about the culture that produced these artifacts.

II. Crete in the Bronze Age.

    **A.** Palatial Society.

        **1.** The scale of architectural complexity in Bronze Age Crete, from 1900–1400 B.C., is unlike anything previously seen in the Greek world, and it has earned the label of "palatial society."

2. The palaces share similarities of design and construction, including a throne room, a ceremonial court, private chambers, storage magazines, controlled points of entry, and multiple levels.

3. Taken together, these point to a highly complex, centralized, and hierarchical society.

**B.** Minoan religion. The palaces were also part of a complex religious system that included cave sanctuaries, house sanctuaries, and mountain sanctuaries.

1. The belief system behind these structures remains difficult to reconstruct, since we have no sacred texts. However, the figurines, shrines, and cult objects suggest a profound reverence for the forces of the natural world.

2. The paucity of evidence can lead to imaginative conclusions. For instance, the presence of goddess figurines and frescoes has led some to suggest that the Cretans held Chthonic beliefs, although very little hard evidence supports this view.

3. We can say with assurance that Minoan culture was sensitive to human beauty and to the beauty of the natural world.

**C.** Redistributive Economy.

1. At the same time, palatial society depended on a firm control of economic production, both in the sphere of staples such as grain, wool, and oil, and in more specialized areas such as perfume, metalwork, and international trade.

2. By controlling production, storage, and redistribution, Minoan palaces placed themselves at the very center of every aspect of daily life.

**III.** A Bronze Age Commonwealth?

**A.** The objects found in excavations, such as seals, scarabs, and rings, show that the Cretans were in contact with many other cultures to the east, notably the Egyptians.

**B.** Cretan influence can also be seen in the Aegean islands, especially Thera, where the Cretans traded and perhaps established colonies. Between 1700 and 1500 B.C., the Cretans were the western-most segment of a Bronze Age world that connected the entire eastern Mediterranean.

**C.** The Minoan palaces were unfortified, which supports the view that the Cretans relied for their defense on naval power, not on land forces.

**IV.** Sir Arthur Evans and the rediscovery of Minoan Crete.

    **A.** The discovery of Cretan culture results from the work of one man, Sir Arthur Evans. Fascinated by clay tablets with an undeciphered script, Evans excavated at Knossos in central Crete, where his workmen immediately began uncovering the remains of the largest and most important Minoan palaces.

    **B.** Evans' discoveries are an excellent example of 19th-century archaeology. Like Schliemann at Troy and Layard at Nineveh, Evans was not a professional scholar. Instead, he was guided by Greek traditions that remembered Crete as the home of a powerful naval empire that existed long before the classical age.

    **C.** Evans' work continues to pose questions for archaeologists. To what extent must the archaeologist rely on written sources? Can archaeology recover the history of a society that has left no literature? Or, as many archaeologists now claim, is archaeology a completely separate discipline from history, with its own methods and discourse?

**Suggested Readings**

Warren, P. (1989) *The Aegean Civilizations*. New York.

Marinatos, N. (1984) *Art and Religion in Thera*. Athens: Ekdotike Athenon.

**Question to Consider**

1. In what ways is the civilization of Minoan Crete comparable to other Bronze Age cultures of the ancient Near East?

2. Is there sufficient evidence to regard Minoan Crete as a theocratic society?

# Lecture Two—Transcript
## Minoan Crete

Welcome back to our series of lectures on Ancient Greek Civilization. In this, the second of the lectures, we're going to be looking at the first really great Bronze Age culture that the Greek world produced. The Greeks actually produced two, more than most other civilizations. Today, we're just going to concentrate on the culture of Minoan Crete. In another lecture, we'll look at Mycenae and the Bronze Age culture of the mainland.

Minoan Crete is a culture that produces quite extraordinary artifacts. We have examples here of quite astonishing city planning. We will have beautiful objects of exquisite craftsmanship. We will find an aesthetic sensibility which is second to none anywhere in the world at any time, and yet we're also going to be looking at a culture that left us no literature. That makes it an extremely puzzling and mysterious culture to examine. That's probably been responsible for some of the more outrageous fantasies about the Minoan world.

Today, we're going to try to separate some of the fact and some of the fantasy about Minoan Crete. Before we start looking at the Bronze Age, and the world particularly of the second millennium B.C. in Greece and Crete, we need to go back a little further to set the stage, just so that we know what's been going on in Greece and to know about human culture in the Greek world.

We have a couple of sites that we can mention that give us an idea of the progress and development of human culture in the Greek world. One of the earliest sites that's supported as evidence goes back to the Stone Age. Here at the Franchthi Cave, which is located in the Argolid, we have evidence for hunters and gatherers living in a cave. What's very interesting about this old Stone Age culture is that we can tell that already, at the very beginning of Greek history—or Greek pre-history, literally—these people are trading and traveling across the water. The evidence for that is absolutely straightforward and it is that in the cave at Franchthi, we have examples of volcanic glass, obsidian, which is used to create blades and arrowheads. This volcanic glass we know comes from the island of Melos. For it to get to the mainland, somebody had to be in a boat traveling across the water.

If we fast-forward to the fifth and fourth millennia B.C., we have evidence for quite complex human societies and social organization at Sesklo and Dimini in central-northern Greece by Thessaly. The remains here are extremely interesting because we have large stone walls made out of field stones protecting the settlements. We have a clear enough idea of the layout of the settlement to see that there seems to have been a chieftain's house in the center and at the uppermost level of the settlement. This is good evidence for a complex society going back that early.

The first culture that really makes an extraordinary impact on us, however, for its cultural production is the civilization that is often called "Cycladic," for the simple reason that the evidence for this culture comes from the Cyclades, the islands of the central Aegean. Yet here we face one of the most frustrating aspects of dealing with archaeological material. Many of you have probably seen Cycladic figurines. These are marble figurines about a foot high. They are highly stylized, usually showing broad shoulders and narrow hips, with sometimes some suggestion of the genitals being depicted, either the woman's breasts or genitals. But we know virtually nothing about the society that produced these.

Aesthetically, they are gorgeous, but what they bring home to us is that an object on its own, outside of an archaeological context, tells you nothing. You can go to the Goulandris Museum in Athens and you will see case after case of these most beautiful objects made sometime between 2800–2300 B.C., but in the vast majority of cases, we know nothing about where exactly it was found or the context in which it was found. Therefore, we can say nothing further about the culture that produced it. It is a pretty object and very little more than that.

Let's turn aside, though, after Cycladic civilization and move into the second millennium B.C. It's now, beginning around 1900 B.C. on the island of Crete, that we have evidence for this extraordinary Bronze Age culture that we know as Minoan culture. Here on Crete, between approximately 1900–1400 B.C., what we're faced with is a series of palaces. This is usually called "palatial society." These palaces share similarities of design and it's important to understand how this design is repeated time and again at the various Minoan sites. We have Knossos, the major one of these Minoan palaces;

Mallia; Phaistos; Kato Zakro; and various others, such as Thassos, for example, on the southern coast.

In each of these places, you will find essentially the same design being repeated. You will find a central courtyard. Around the central courtyard on one side, you will normally find a series of administrative buildings with, for example, throne rooms, interview rooms and sometimes a ritual bath as well. Then, on another side of the ceremonial courtyard, you will normally find a series of private chambers, sumptuously decorated. In the case of Knossos, we have examples of the beautiful frescoes which were used to decorate these.

Then, usually on one side of the courtyard behind the administrative buildings, we also have a third important feature of these Minoan palaces. These are the so-called "magazines": magazines used in the sense of storage rooms. If you're very lucky and you go into one of these, you may even still find "pithoi" in place. These pithoi are often six-foot tall vases or storage vessels that were made right there in place. The fact that we have room after room with dozens of these tells us that what we have here is the palace acting as an economic center as well.

These palaces are really the core to understanding Minoan culture. They are administrative centers. They are religious centers and they are economic centers. Let's take each of these a little further. In the case of Knossos, one archaeologist some years ago wrote a wonderful remark when he said that he was not sure that the bottom which sat in the throne at the throne room at Knossos wasn't female. We may have here some matriarchal or matrilineal society, but it's very difficult to know for sure.

Later Greek myth, of course, associated the power of this culture of Crete with the legendary king, Minos. That's why we refer to it as Minoan culture. We should entertain the possibility that perhaps it was a matriarchal society and that it was a woman who was the queen and the most powerful person at Knossos.

We can also say about these palaces that they show similarities of design to palaces that are found throughout the ancient Near East. What we're finding here is an idea of social organization and an idea of social order which has begun in those ancient cultures of the Near

East—Sumer, Babylon, Ugarit and so forth—and which is now finding expression in the Greek world.

We can go a little bit further. Here the interesting topic that we should address is that of Minoan religion. The palaces were clearly the center of—or at least a part of—an extremely complex religious system. We know, for example, that the Minoans also worshiped on mountaintops. We have mountaintop sanctuaries that have been excavated and mountaintop sanctuaries that are shown in Minoan art. We know of house sanctuaries where various goddess figurines have been found. The bell-shaped figurines show the goddess in her long dress with her little feet poking out. We have these house sanctuaries, and we also have cave sanctuaries, where often literally hundreds of small figurines have been found, dedications to the god worshiped there.

The palaces are part of this system as well. That we can be fairly sure of, particularly when we look at the wonderful decoration of the walls of the Minoan palaces. Here we will often see princes marching forward with dedicatory offerings or priestesses accepting offerings on their behalf. We also know of performances and rituals carried out in these courtyards at the center of the palaces that almost certainly had some kind of religious significance.

For example, in one of the most remarkable frescoes to come to us from the Minoan world, we see two athletes at either end of a bull, one appearing to steady its rump and the other to be steadying its horns as a third athlete leaps over the horns of the bull and vaults over its back. This is quite an astonishing performance and it recalls the close association that the bull has for many cultures (and it certainly seems to be the case here) with divine power and virility. We seem to have this performance taking place in the palaces representing some kind of athletic performance and homage to some kind of virile deity.

You'll notice that as I talk about this Minoan religion, what I'm doing here is often talking about archaeological sites or objects and trying to extract a meaning from it. If I were talking about a modern culture and I wanted to discuss its religion, of course the first thing I would do would be to go to a religious text. One of the problems that bedevils the study of the Bronze Age is that we are dealing with a society in Minoan Crete that has left us no literature. There is no religious literature and there is no liturgy. We can sing no hymns to these gods or goddesses. There is no secular literature either—no love poems.

It's very difficult to reconstruct the mentality or the thought world or the world of belief that surrounds this Minoan culture. Instead, what we have to rely on is extrapolation from the archaeological and the iconographic evidence.

Such extrapolations can be a little dangerous. I want to give you one example. You may have seen the fresco that is often referred to as "the Prince," a figure shown in a hieratic stance, a young man with a great plumed headdress who seems to be either a priest or a powerful figure in Minoan culture, shown on the walls at Knossos. Like nearly all the other depictions, either in wall paintings, frescoes or even in the minor arts of Minoan men, he's wearing a characteristic outfit usually referred to as a kilt. It appears to be a heavy leather belt around his midriff and then some kind of cloth kilt that goes down from that.

Some years ago, it was argued that the reason that the men shown in all Minoan art are so handsome, manly and virile looking, is that when they reached their adulthood, they were actually welded into one of these garments. It was a metal band and they were not physically capable of growing any fatter as they got older because the garment wouldn't allow them to. Of course, there is absolutely no evidence for this. There is no literary evidence for it and in fact, it's probably a silly idea right from the very beginning. But it illustrates the way in which Minoan culture, because it is in a sense a silent culture, has allowed people to imagine it to be something else.

The presence of goddess figurines has led many people to suppose that we have here some earth religion that deals with the power of the feminine principle. In fact, all we can say is that we know we have many of these figurines, which show the Minoan goddess or priestess wearing the typical garments of the Minoan woman. That is, the tight blouse leaving the breasts exposed, the long flounced skirt (we see these in frescoes and figurines), and in the case of many of these goddess or priestess figurines, we see snakes entwined around the arms. Snakes are traditionally associated with the earth and with regeneration as they slough their skin. They're often associated with ancestor worship as well.

What was the precise meaning of the snake in Minoan religion? We don't know. All we can do is by analogy suggest that we have here a religious system which incorporates the world, the earth, and the ground, possibly construed as a female principle (the lady Greeks certainly thought of it as the Earth Mother, Demeter, the Earth Mother).

Then we seem to have some kind of sky god being worshiped in these hilltop shrines. It may be that we have, given the fact that our palaces here look like palaces from the ancient Near East, something like the same pattern that we find in those cultures as well, where often a powerful female goddess has a male consort. This remains imbedded in the ancient Near East in many of its gods and goddesses. It even goes down later into Greek and Roman myth and is remembered in stories, for example that of Venus and Adonis.

It may be—it *may* be, I emphasize—that on Crete, we had an Earth Mother and we had a virile male consort, but I can't give you their names. I cannot give you a single line of any hymn sung in their honor at all. All we can do is extrapolate from silent archaeological evidence and analogous evidence from other places. Some of these, I think, are a fairly safe bet.

Normally, I wouldn't talk in terms of aesthetics because this is so subjective, but what we can say is that we have very clear evidence that this Minoan culture was an extraordinarily sensitive culture—a culture that was alive to the beauty of the natural world around it. It was also alive to human beauty as well. One of the most famous frescoes excavated at Knossos is one which Sir Arthur Evans' excavators turned up soon after they had started digging. When they found this piece of plaster with the head of a woman shown in profile with her ruby red lipstick and her hair pulled back into a gorgeous hairdo, she was dubbed "La Parisienne" ("the Parisian girl") because she looks like a beautiful girl of the Parisian demimonde at the turn of the century.

We have very many other frescoes that similarly show elegant, beautiful Minoan women and young handsome Minoan men. This is obviously in some respects an idealized version of what their society is. I presume there were some old and wrinkled Minoans somewhere, but we don't see many of them in our evidence. What instead we see is a culture which was alive to beauty and liked to decorate its walls with motifs such as dolphins, and to show the beauty of the sea—the sea that the Minoans were themselves trading in as they made their way around the eastern Mediterranean.

This brings us, then, to the other aspects of the palaces that I've touched upon. In addition to being administrative centers, political centers and centers of power, and in addition to being associated with this religious system of ideas, they are also the center of the economy. This is really a critical part of Minoan society. Minoan culture is often referred to as a "redistributive economy." What we mean by that is that the palaces serve as a nodal point. Produce from the surrounding countryside—staples such as grain, wool and oil—is brought in from the countryside and stored in these great pithoi in the magazines. Then in turn, they are redistributed out to people as they need them.

In addition to this control of the staple economy, it also looks as if the palaces, as you would expect since they are the homes of the elite (the kings, queens, princes and so forth), are the center of an international trade. It's in these palaces that we will find examples of perfume; metal being brought in in its raw state and turned into beautifully worked metal objects; fabrics being imported from the outside world; precious woods from the eastern Mediterranean; spices, and these sorts of things.

Farmers are not trading these up in the mountains. These are being brought in for princes. They are stored here and then redistributed out. We can think of the palaces as being the center in every respect—in all parts—of Minoan life.

I've been referring both to national trade in staples and the goods produced around Knossos and around Mallia, where farmers are probably under the control of or closely connected to the palace, but also this international trade—goods coming in from overseas. It's from these excavations in Crete that we find conclusive evidence that the Cretans were in contact with many of the other great cultures of the eastern Mediterranean during the Bronze Age. In other words, you will find scarabs and pieces of lapis lazuli. You will find seals and rings made of gold or cut from amber that were made in other parts of the eastern Mediterranean, such as Mesopotamia, Syria, Cyprus and Egypt, and made their way to Crete.

In a way, we should change our focus. Instead of thinking of Crete as the first Greek Bronze Age culture, let's think of it in these terms: as being the farthest west of the whole range of Bronze Age cultures which existed over the eastern Mediterranean in the second half of the second millennium B.C.

The word that is sometimes used to describe this is the "*oikoumene*" (the "commonwealth" or "shared world"). If we think in those terms, really what we're getting in Crete is the farthest western expression of a style of culture and civilization, based on international trade and an export of ideas as well as objects, that links Mesopotamia, Syria, Egypt—the entire Levant or eastern Mediterranean—and Crete.

We see, I think, some of the best evidence for this not just on Crete itself, but on the island of Thera. We'll be talking more about that in another lecture, because Thera is going to become very important for our explanation of what happened to the Cretans. On the island of Thera, what we fairly clearly have is a society that is closely linked to Crete. Was it a Cretan colony or is it an indigenous society that is heavily influenced by Crete? It's hard to answer that exactly, but what we can see in this island in the objects found here—particularly in the wall paintings found on Thera—is that this island was part of a Cretan network—a trade network and a cultural network.

The reason I emphasize this is, I think, quite important. Some of the more fantastic explanations of Cretan power and culture have pointed to the fact that in Crete we do not find, generally speaking, walls around the palaces. Think about this for a moment. If you live in a world where there are marauders and pirates and you choose not to build walls around your palace, you're making quite a statement of your power.

In the past, people have sometimes said this is conclusive evidence that we have here a peace-loving culture—a culture of feminine power that didn't feel the need to build surrounding walls or to be militaristic and protect its cities. In fact, I would suggest the explanation is quite different. It is that the defense of Crete was not on Cretan soil. It was out there in the islands. The defense of Crete came with its naval power. I would point out to you that, for example, that's exactly what the Greeks of hundreds of years later remembered about Minoan Crete: that it had been remarkable for the strength of its naval power.

Thucydides says: "Minos was the first to build a great fleet." In that, I think what we're getting is some memory of the fact that the

Cretans didn't need to defend their own soil throughout most of their history, because for most of the time, they could defend it with their fleets sailing out around the eastern Mediterranean and the Aegean.

There's one other aspect of Crete that I want to discuss briefly and I think this is something that we might want to keep in mind during some of the future lectures. One of my abiding interests is the question of how do we know what we claim to know about a particular culture? Minoan Crete is particularly instructive in that respect, because this is one place where we can say quite definitively we owe everything almost to one man: his name is Sir Arthur Evans.

Evans was a journalist who had traveled around the eastern Mediterranean and while in Greece and on Crete, he was shown certain pieces of clay with glyphs (writing) on them that had not been translated. Fascinated by these tablets, he tried to find where they'd been found. He then went and, in the good practice of the late 19th/early 20th century, he bought the land where they'd been found.

Shortly after, he set an excavation team to work. The site from which these tablets came, and which he partially purchased and then excavated, is Knossos, the type site that we've been considering in everything we have to say about the palatial culture of Minoan Crete. We owe most of what we know about Minoan Crete, and Knossos in particular, to the work of this one man, Sir Arthur Evans, a monumental intellect and a monumental influence on the archaeology of the Bronze Age. Within days of beginning the excavations, his workmen were turning up hundreds of tablets in a script which unfortunately, I have to say, is still not substantially translated: Linear A.

I want to make a few points about Evans and about the kind of archaeology that he was doing. We need, I think, to keep these in mind. Evans' discoveries are good examples of 19th century and early 20th century archaeology at work. Like Schliemann at Troy and Mycenae and like Layard at Nineveh, Evans was not a professional scholar. He was not a university professor who'd been trained in Greek and Latin He didn't teach these at a university at all. Rather, he was a man of the world that, like many of the best educated in the 19th century, had been immersed in the world of the Greeks and classical culture.

With him, as with these other archaeologists, it was a passion to find the real objects that attested the reality of that world, which otherwise was only known through myth, epic and the work of the later Greek historians. He was guided by these Greek traditions (the ones we've already alluded to), which remembered Crete as the home of King Minos and of a powerful naval empire.

The reason I raise all this is for this purpose. Archaeology has come a long way in the generations since Evans. We now deal with more elaborate models and try to explain the growth, change, decline and operation of various cultures. None of this could have occurred in our study of the Bronze Age had there not been originally a handful of men with fire in their belly to go out, to get off their backsides, and simply to put a shovel into the ground.

While in some ways it's almost a cheap shot to say these early archaeologists often destroyed before they recorded properly, their notebooks can be difficult to read, or there can be questions as to the veracity of some of their discoveries (you're surely familiar with the fact that Schliemann has been attacked by many on these grounds). It's easy in hindsight to attack the shortcomings of these men, but on the other hand, we owe them a great deal. We owe them everything in fact. Without them, we wouldn't even have a Bronze Age discipline.

There's one other aspect of Evans' work that I want to really finish with today. It's a problem that I alluded to a little bit earlier and it's this: in the case of Minoan Crete, we have no literary records. We have no historian of Minoan Crete. We have no religious liturgy. We have no lyric poetry. We have no epic poetry. It raises, I think, an extremely interesting question for the historian: to what degree can the historian really reliably recreate a past civilization when it is essentially a mute civilization?

That's not a simple question. It's one that became very important for me the first time I saw some of these frescoes at Knossos—these beautiful frescoes. When you actually see them up close, you will realize that while you may be looking at a figure which is six feet tall shown in a particular hieratic position and beautifully painted, of that six feet, often six inches is original and five and a half feet are restored.

When you go to Knossos, which is one of the world heritage archaeological sites, how much are you seeing that is truly Bronze Age and how much are you seeing that is Evans' perhaps intelligent, perhaps inspired reconstruction of that culture? It's a troubling question.

There are many archaeologists who will tell you quite simply, citing their mantra, "Archaeology is archaeology is archaeology," by which they mean that regardless of what your literary sources tell you, you must simply go with what the archaeology shows you. To a certain degree that is true and to a certain degree we're tied to that, because we have so few literary sources for the Minoan world. But where we don't have literary sources, we are still thrown back on interpretation, and the interpretation in this case of one particularly great and powerful man.

I praise, therefore, like Brutus over the body of Caesar, Sir Arthur Evans for what he gave us in his work at Knossos. But in another lecture, we're going to see that part of his legacy also was to hold back the archaeology of the Bronze Age, as he posited a relationship between Minoan Crete and the second great Bronze Age culture of Greece, that of the Mycenaean world on the mainland. The details of that we will get to in the next lecture.

# Lecture Three
# Schliemann and Mycenae

**Scope:**

The second great Bronze Age culture of Greece takes its name from the site of Mycenae, excavated first by Heinrich Schliemann. Taking Homer as his guide, Schliemann uncovered the traces of a powerful warrior society. Unlike the Cretan palaces, the site of Mycenae and other sites of the same period—Tiryns, Gla, and Orchomenos, for example—were protected by massive walls of Cyclopean masonry. Grave goods from Mycenaean sites point to a warrior élite whose trading contacts reached to Crete and beyond, to Egypt and Syria.

At many of these sites, tablets in a script known as Linear B were found. In 1954 Michael Ventris demonstrated that the language of Linear B was a form of Greek. This discovery was of enormous importance, since it helped to establish, after more than 50 years of debate, the relationship between the civilization of Minoan Crete and the Mycenaeans.

# Outline

**I.** Mysterious Origins.

    **A.** When in 1876 Schliemann uncovered traces of a wealthy society at Mycenae, he believed that he had found the homeland of Homer's Achaians, the Greeks who had sacked Troy.

        **1.** Subsequent work has shown that he had brought to light a civilization whose roots go back to the middle of the second millennium B.C.

        **2.** Schliemann's Mycenae, like Homer's, was "rich in gold." The origins of this gold, as well as the power of the Mycenaeans, remains mysterious.

    **B.** It is likely that the Mycenaeans' ancestors first entered the Greek peninsula around 1900 B.C., but the early phases of the culture's development are hard to trace. By the 16th and 15th centuries B.C. they were already burying their chieftains in deep shaft graves with rich grave goods, including gold death masks and ceremonial swords of bronze inlaid with silver.

## II. An Elite Culture.

**A.** The material culture left by the Mycenaeans evokes a world dominated by an élite class.

  **1.** Massive fortifications, swords, and gems showing warriors in battle or hunting lions point towards the martial prowess of the Mycenaeans.

  **2.** Their grave goods also show a taste for luxury. Finely worked jewelry in gold and precious stones and sumptuous drinking vessels illustrate the wealth of the Mycenaean world.

**B.** Since Schliemann's time, excavations have added to our knowledge of the Mycenaeans in two important respects.

  **1.** In the first place, we now know that many Mycenaean sites functioned like Minoan palaces. Artisans crafting luxury items in precious metals and workers making perfume lived either within the fortresses or directly below, making the Mycenaean sites proto-towns.

  **2.** Furthermore, many of the vessels, jewels, and frescoes enjoyed by the Mycenaeans reveal the influence of other, older cultures, especially Crete.

## III. Cultures in Conflict.

**A.** The deep influence of Minoan culture on the Mycenaean world prompted a long debate.

  **1.** According to Sir Arthur Evans, it was the Cretans who had colonized the mainland. Mycenae was an off-shoot of Crete.

  **2.** Others argued that the Mycenaeans had an indigenous Greek culture that came under the influence of Cretan style through trade and eventually through the conquest of Crete.

**B.** This debate was finally resolved by the translation of Linear B, the script used in the Mycenaean fortresses to keep accounts of property, such as sheep, chariot parts, and slaves. In 1954 Michael Ventris demonstrated that Linear B was a form of Greek.

**C.** The relationship between Crete and Mycenae is now clearer.

  **1.** Around 1450 the Cretan palaces were destroyed. Only Knossos was rebuilt; it flourished for another 75 years.

2. The records from Knossos during this last occupation were recorded in Linear B, not the script used earlier on Crete, which we call Linear A. Since Linear B is Greek, it looks as if Greek speakers occupied Knossos in its last phase. These Greeks from the mainland invaded and occupied Knossos and stayed for three generations, long enough to learn the practice of a centralized palatial economy.

D. Other data confirm the theory that Greeks from the mainland overwhelmed the Cretans.
   1. At Miletus and on Rhodes, Cretan colonies founded by the Minoans shortly after 1600 B.C. had come into the hands of the Mycenaeans by 1400 B.C.
   2. The myth of Theseus and the Minotaur may be a distant memory of this conflict between the mainland and Crete.

## Suggested Reading

Traill, D.A. (1993) *Excavating Schliemann*. Illinois Classical Studies, Supplement 4. Atlanta: Scholar's Press.

## Questions to Consider

1. Can Greek myths be used to reconstruct the world of the Bronze Age?
2. What is the significance of Ventris' discovery that Linear B is a form of Greek?

# Lecture Three—Transcript
## Schliemann and Mycenae

Welcome back to our series of lectures on Ancient Greek Civilization. In the last lecture, we looked at the world of Minoan Crete, the first of the two great Bronze Age civilizations that we have from the Greek world. At the end of that lecture, I was talking about Sir Arthur Evans and suggesting that Evans was in a way the creator of what we know about that Bronze Age culture. When you look at the frescoes at Knossos, we see not just what was there, but also the restorations done by Evans and his draughtsmen.

When we turn to the second of the great Bronze Age cultures, that of Mycenaean Greece, the Bronze Age culture of the mainland, we find yet again that we are beholden to the work of one great archaeologist. Like Evans, the great archaeologist who uncovered for us Mycenaean Greece, Heinrich Schliemann, was not a professional scholar. In fact, he was anything but. He had been a businessman in the early part of his life. He had made a fortune on the California gold fields, not by digging for gold, but rather by providing goods to the gold diggers. The fortune that he made allowed him as a middle aged man to turn his attention to his true love, which was the world of Homer—the epic world of the Greeks.

Armed with Homer as his guide, he quite simply set off to find the places which Homer had described and the places which had been the homeland of those Bronze Age Greeks whom Homer called the "Achaians." When in 1876 he excavated at Mycenae, he uncovered the traces of a glorious Bronze Age culture, a wealthy society which he took to be the homeland of Homer's Mycenaean Greeks, the Achaians.

In fact, there's a wonderful story told of Schliemann's work at Mycenae. He first came across two grave circles and within these grave circles, he was able to find a number of shaft graves that had been dug down through the soil and into the rock. At the bottom of one of these, having excavated all the material above, he came down upon what he claimed to be the remains of one of Homer's Achaian kings. Of course, the great king who ruled at Mycenae in Homer's poems is Agamemnon. When Schliemann got to the bottom of this shaft grave, he came upon a gold mask, a death mask, which had been placed over the ancient king. According to Schliemann and a telegram that he later sent, when he lifted the gold faceplate off, for a second he saw the face of Agamemnon.

It's a wonderful story and in a way, it sums up everything that is both wonderful and terrible about Schliemann. That is to say, his flair for the dramatic and his understanding of what would excite his audience made archaeology internationally famous and the culture of the Greeks internationally famous, yet there is always a question of how much was fabricated by this very gifted storyteller (I don't mean Homer, I mean Schliemann).

Subsequent work carried on at Mycenae by generations of British, Greek and American archaeologists has added more nuance to the story of what Schliemann originally found. We now know that the civilization which he uncovered in the shaft graves was in fact a civilization flourishing around 1600–1500 B.C., some 300–400 years earlier than the supposed date of the Trojan War, which Schliemann thought that he was uncovering archaeologically. In fact, he was down even below the levels of Agamemnon or Priam and excavating something earlier: a Bronze Age culture located in the mainland of Greece that was already reaching a peak of wealth and power after 1600 B.C.

The grave goods that came from the shaft graves are extraordinarily rich and they justify the label that Homer gave to Mycenae, which is "Mycenae, rich in gold." They also create a problem for us, because Greece is not rich in gold. The question arises, "Where did this material wealth come from?" If it was not excavated in Greece itself, then it was brought in from elsewhere. If so, then we are dealing with a major international power in the middle of the second millennium B.C.—a Mycenaean Greece that was part of this broader Bronze Age *oikoumene*, or commonwealth, that I described in earlier lectures.

It raises the question also of the origins of these Mycenaean Greeks. Who were these people? Where did they come from? You will notice that I'm calling them Greeks throughout. That's justified by the fact that, as we're going to see a little bit later on, we know that the language that they were speaking and recording was in fact a form of Greek.

The question, though, of when they originate in Greece is slightly more complex. Archaeologists point to a very abrupt change in the archaeological record of Greece around 1900 B.C. That abrupt change includes for the first time the appearance of a kind of pottery that was found originally in Anatolia. What do we make of that? That might mean that people coming from Anatolia (what is modern day Turkey) across northern Greece and the Aegean descended into Greece. It would make sense if they were the first Greek speakers, bringing their Indo-European language with them.

Another datum that helps us here is that of the Greek language itself, because, interestingly, Greek has within it traces of an earlier language which is not Indo-European. There are place names, such as Corinth and Tiryns, where the names themselves, linguists tell us, are not Greek. There are every day objects and parts of every day life in Greece such as mint (*menta*) and ivy (*kissos*), the words for which do not fit into the broader Greek language and are not a part of it— they're non-Indo-European.

We seem to have, then, traces of a non-Greek people in Greece. Then, we have, around 1900, a fairly abrupt transition archaeologically. It would make sense if that's the origin of the Greeks in Greece around 1900 B.C.

What was going on with these people in Greece between their arrival and the sudden flowering of Mycenaean power around 1600-1500 B.C.? The answer is we basically don't know. The record is very patchy. All that we can really say is that by about 1600–1500 B.C., the people living at Mycenae, who were almost certainly Greek speakers, were burying their chieftains in deep shaft graves and honoring them with extraordinarily rich burial or funeral offerings, which included, for example, extraordinarily elaborate ceremonial swords made of bronze and inlaid with silver. It's fairly clear that what we have at Mycenae in the middle of the second millennium B.C. is an elite culture—a culture dominated by an elite class.

As soon as you start looking at the objects produced by the Mycenaean world and compare it to the earlier world of Crete, the other Bronze Age culture, you find that there are quite remarkable differences that are immediately apparent. For example, if you go to Knossos on Crete, as we've seen before, you find no fortification walls. You can walk straight to one of the entrances and, making your way around the labyrinthian passages, come out to the central courtyard and the throne room.

Go to Mycenae, and you are faced with a magnificent bastion made of such extraordinarily large stones that the Greeks of later ages believed that it was impossible for humans to have built these walls. They must have been built by giants or by those great gigantic craftsmen, the Cyclops, so we call these walls "Cyclopean walls." It's not a terrifically technical term at all. It simply means the Greeks thought they weren't able to do it and it must have been done by someone superhuman.

When we see these massive fortifications, when we see the swords being buried with these chieftains, when we see the grave stones marking their graves with their chariots, and when we see these warriors in battle as they're shown on the sword blades, either fighting other warriors or fighting heroically against lions and cutting them down, what we see over and over again is the martial quality of Mycenaean culture. This was a warrior culture—of that I have no doubt.

It is also, however, a culture with a great taste for luxury. We find finely worked vessels made of alabastron and other stones. We find extraordinarily fine gold work, often showing not just geometric designs beaten out of the gold repoussé, but also designs that show scenes of hunters and farmers taming wild bulls, and other scenes of this sort. We have sumptuous drinking vessels and collectively all this evidence points to a wealthy Mycenaean world and one with a great taste for luxury.

In the 120 years or so since Schliemann's excavations at Mycenae, the rest of the excavations there have added to our knowledge of the Mycenaeans in two very important respects. The first is that we know that at the end of its history in the 13th century B.C. in particular, Mycenae was functioning very much like a Minoan palace. It had these monumental walls, but we've found, sometimes within the bastion but sometimes outside as well, signs of craftsmen and workers living below the palace. The men and women who worked with precious metals or who made perfume were living in a kind of proto-town, as it were.

It looks as if in some ways Mycenae was reflecting the influence of the Minoan world. The other thing that we know quite clearly from this century's excavations is that stylistically the Mycenaean world was borrowing extremely heavily from Minoan Crete. That is to say, Minoan vessels (either made in Crete and exported to Greece or made in Mycenae by Minoan craftsmen—on loan perhaps, or itinerant craftsmen, who knows?) are turning up in a Mycenaean city. Mycenaean culture, though a native Greek culture—indigenous, if you will—is strongly affected by its contact with the world of Crete. It is borrowing its motifs. It is modeling itself on them.

We are familiar in the modern world with this sort of cultural movement. If you think, for example, of the way that Japan has become increasingly westernized in the period since the Second World War, you see this kind of cultural influence turning up in the way people dress, in the kind of vessels they use, and so forth.

This relationship between the Minoan world, a brilliant Bronze Age culture, and the Mycenaean world, another brilliant Bronze Age culture, creates a debate—a debate that dominated the archaeology of the pre-historic period throughout the early part of this century. The positions are relatively clear. Sir Arthur Evans, the founder, creator and rediscoverer, if you will, of Knossos, maintained that the line of transmission was very simple: Crete was the mother culture and the Cretans colonized the mainland, so that the culture of the mainland, though it has local and indigenous elements, is essentially an off-shoot of Cretan culture and Cretan colonists.

Others, particularly Alan Wace, the English excavator in the first part of the century, argued that in fact Mycenaean Greece had been a separate culture—an indigenous culture which had come under Cretan influence, not by colonization by the Cretans, but by its exposure to Cretan artwork and Cretan style, particularly as a result of trading contacts out in the islands and in the Aegean.

This debate was resolved triumphantly in the early 1950s. The event, which resolved this debate, was, in my humble opinion, the most significant event in Greek archaeology this century. It was not an excavation. It was the translation of Linear B by the English architect Michael Ventris, who demonstrated conclusively that Linear B is Greek.

Let me explain the significance of this and relate it to the question of the two cultures. We have seen that on Crete, we have a palatial culture going back to about 1900 B.C. The palaces there underwent a period of destruction around 1700 B.C., but they were rebuilt very shortly afterwards. Most of the Minoan palaces went through a second period, then, of prosperity that lasted from about 1700–1450

B.C. At that point, they underwent a second destruction from which very few survived or recovered. In fact, only one did: Knossos.

For about 75 years (these dates are very approximate—they're based generally on pottery sequences, so they're not absolutely concrete), from about 1450–1375 B.C., the palace of Knossos was once again inhabited. The people who inhabited it during that last period, three generations approximately, kept records as had the Minoans of earlier generations. But the records that they kept turned out to be not in Linear A, the earlier script used in Crete, but in a new script, Linear B.

Linear B turns up on a number of mainland sites as well, particularly around 1200 B.C. at Pylos, Mycenae and other Mycenaean sites. Ventris, by successfully cracking the code of Linear B, was able to show that Linear B was the language being used by the Mycenaean groups. If it occurred in Crete during its last phase, then it follows that Mycenaean Greeks occupied Knossos in its final phase. Far from suggesting that it was Crete which had colonized the mainland, this argument seemed to suggest that Mycenaean culture had grown up independently, had been under the influence of Cretan culture, but then at some pivotal point, the relationship between the two had changed. In the middle of the 15th century B.C., around 1450 B.C., it was Mycenaean power which became dominant and eventually even overthrew the culture of Minoan Crete.

That was quite a breathtaking discovery and yet it seems to have been confirmed by subsequent work. For example, if you look at various sites from the middle of the second millennium B.C. around the eastern Aegean, such as Miletus and Rhodes, what you find around 1600 B.C. is essentially Minoan pottery. In other words, these places are either Minoan colonies, Minoan trading ports or places where Minoan fleets pull in and do business. We can't specify exactly the relationship, but they're largely within the Minoan sphere of influence.

Excavate those same sites to the levels that occur 200 years later (or 200 years above, if you will) and what you find is that the pottery is not Minoan—it's Mycenaean. In other words, between 1600 B.C. and 1400 B.C., there has been a very dramatic change in the control of the Aegean and even of the wider eastern Mediterranean, which at an earlier stage had been largely under a Cretan influence, but by 1400 B.C. was now decidedly under a Mycenaean influence.

There is another bit of evidence that we need to bring to bear on this, one that I feel somewhat dubious about, but I want to throw it out for your consideration. The Greeks of later times remembered a story involving one of the greatest heroes of Greece, particularly an Athenian hero, by the name of Theseus. It's a story that you all know and that story is that every year, the Athenians were asked to send seven youths and seven maidens in homage to Minos, the King of Crete. These seven youths and seven maidens were then sacrificed in the Labyrinth to a hideous creature called the Minotaur. The Minotaur was a creature that was half man and half bull—half bull and half son of Minos if you like (or half descended from).

According to the myth recalled by these later Greeks, Theseus, after falling in love with Ariadne and enlisting her help, is able, in fact, to negotiate the Labyrinth, successfully kill the Minotaur, come back out, liberate the Athenian youths, and then set sail back for Athens.

I want you to consider for a moment, whether there is a way that we can peel away what we might call the "mytho-poetic," the storytelling element in this, and try to get back to what may be a historical kernel. You may think me simpleminded for this, but I believe that we can. The way I would do it is as follows. It would seem to me that in the story of the Labyrinth, we clearly have some kind of memory of an extraordinary structure. In fact, it's the palace at Knossos. If you've gone to Knossos and you've seen its three and four levels of buildings, you see there a structure that would have had an astonishing impact on people had they been living up in the mountains or herding or never seen a city before.

We have to imagine this making an impact on people and them thinking of this as being quite extraordinary. We add to this the notion that we have a Minoan power that doesn't need to build walls because it has a forward defense—that is to say, it has its fleets sailing out around the Aegean and the eastern Mediterranean. We seem to have seen concrete evidence for this in the pottery that we've talked about at Rhodes and at Miletus, and in the wall paintings that we've seen at Thera.

We have these Minoan fleets sailing out around the Aegean establishing colonies, trading posts and asserting the dominion of Crete. One place finally was able to throw off that dominion. There was a revolt. When did it occur? Some time between 1600–1450 B.C. I think that what we have in the story of Theseus is a folk memory, if you will, of that revolt—of the throwing off of Minoan power. In fact, the historical event that really goes with it is the Mycenaean invasion of around 1450 B.C.

We have to imagine, in fact, a kind of trade war that's been going on between the two great Bronze Age powers. It is a Bronze Age world in which at first the Minoans were powerful, but then subsequently the Mycenaeans were able to assert their influence in Greece, in the islands, and then finally even on Crete itself.

That's the basic story, I believe, of the relationship between the two cultures. Since in subsequent lectures we're going to be talking about the historical periods of Greek history when we have literary records to read, I think now's a moment when we need to stop for a moment and look back at the Bronze Age and ask, "What are the elements that we've been relying on to try to reconstruct the world of the Bronze Age?"

We've been using mythology, and there are many people who would worry about that because myths are stories that undergo a great deal of change in transmission. We have to be very careful in the use of myth and we're going to see more about that in the next lecture when we talk about the reasons for the collapse of the Bronze Age completely. Again, I'm going to be relying on Bronze Age stories to bring this into focus.

The use of myth is certainly a problem. Other literary sources? Only the material recorded by the Greeks hundreds of years subsequently. For the most part, in both the case of the Bronze Age on Crete and the Bronze Age in the Mycenaean world, we are relying only on archaeological data. That is data that requires very careful interpretation.

We don't really know a great deal, finally, about the world of the Bronze Age. We are really guessing most of the time. Yet—and this is the final point I want to make and it's really quite an important one—even though we feel as if we don't know a great deal about the Bronze Age, I'd suggest to you that we actually know a great deal more about it than the Greeks did. They had no archaeology. Yes, certainly if you went to Mycenae in the Classical period, you could see that there had been some great building there, but look at the stories they created out of this. It couldn't be human; it was built by the Cyclops.

They didn't develop a historical sense until Herodotus or Thucydides in the fifth century B.C., and even then they really didn't treat very much the antique past, because they had nothing to say about it that was reliable.

We, with our archaeology, have reconstructed some of the Bronze Age, but the Greeks had very little, and yet (and this is very important in my estimation) this is the genius of the Greeks: they're in fact liberated by not having a clear idea of their past. They were free to do something quite different with it, which is to turn it into the world of the imagination. We use history and archaeology to try to get back to what really happened. Freed from the constraints of an accurate knowledge of history, the Greeks instead approached it quite differently, in a way that we could call mytho-poetic. It was a way that was less interested in historical reality and more interested in a poetic memory of the past.

That might sound nice and airy-fairy. What does it mean in concrete terms? What it means is this: for hundreds of years after the Bronze Age, Greek poets were telling stories based on that world. They told stories about the great king at Mycenae, Agamemnon, or the great redheaded king and his horrible queen in Sparta, Menelaus and Helen. They had no accurate knowledge of these people. Instead, what they did was to take some vague memories of that Bronze Age world and to cobble them together into a series of stories and poems, which then took on a life of their own.

Homer and Hesiod, by going back to that world, were actually giving the Greeks something much more important than a sense of history: they were giving them a sense of identity—that this was their heroic past. In one way, we could say that while we examine the Bronze Age of the Greeks, what the Greeks themselves examined was their Golden Age. We call it the Bronze Age because we're dealing with the real metals being used, but in Homer, that world was transformed through memory and through poetry into something much more potent. When we read the *Iliad* and the *Odyssey*, what we are in fact getting is a poetic distillation of 500 years of oral tradition after the Bronze Age—a tradition that kept the memory alive and in every retelling of the story, subtly transformed it, condensed it and distilled it, until it became something pure and essential.

That pure and essential memory finally became much more important for the Greeks than an accurate knowledge of the Bronze

Age. Instead, it became the core of what they were as Greeks. That is why in all subsequent generations, Greek youths—Greek boys—are going to grow up being taught Homer. They're not reading Schliemann, Blegen or Evans. They're not worrying about what is physically to be seen at Mycenae or seeing the Mycenaean palace on the Acropolis at Athens. The physical remnants—the things we've been concerned about—really convey nothing to them. They are merely objects there. Instead, the reinterpretation of that past into something else—into something heroic—will become most important.

What we will do, then, in the next lecture is very quickly look at the specific reasons—we're going to revert to history and archaeology—of why this culture really did collapse. Then what I want to do is go on from there and, through an examination of Homer and the Dark Ages, talk about the material difference between the Bronze Age and what comes after (the Iron Age). Then, we'll explore the way in which, by being released from the dead hand of the past and by not having to concentrate on the accurate knowledge of history, the Greeks were able, through myth, memory and poetry, finally to create something much more lasting: a Greek identity and finally a Greek culture.

# Lecture Four
# The Long Twilight

**Scope:**

Shortly after 1200 B.C., Mycenaean power declined rapidly. The abrupt end of the Bronze Age in Greece has been a vexed issue in Greek archaeology for more than a century. In this lecture, we review the major explanations that have been put forward. The most dramatic explanation is natural disaster. Did a cataclysm, such as a volcanic eruption or tidal wave, cause the collapse of Bronze Age civilization? Or did invasions and military conquests bring an end to the cultures of Crete and Mycenae? A third possibility is that internal revolts toppled societies that were too fragile to resist. Finally, we should ask whether we can find an explanation by looking beyond Greece and Crete to the other cultures of the Bronze Age Mediterranean.

## Outline

I. Thera and the Theory of Volcanic Destruction.

    **A.** The most romantic explanation for the destruction of Minoan Crete is that it was devastated by a volcanic eruption on Thera.

        **1.** Thera lies 200 miles northeast of Crete. It was wiped out by a single, massive volcanic eruption.

        **2.** The excavator Spiridon Marinatos argued that Minoan coastal sites showed evidence of inundation by a massive tidal wave.

        **3.** Plato's later stories of Atlantis seem to recall a civilization destroyed by a natural cataclysm.

    **B.** But there is strong evidence that counts against the volcanic theory.

        **1.** Scientific evidence now dates the eruption close to 1600 B.C., rather than around 1400, when the Cretan palaces were destroyed.

        **2.** Marine-style pottery, not found on Thera, is found on Crete and appears to postdate the Thera eruption.

        **3.** Coastal sites on the Cretan coast at Pseira and Mochlos show signs of habitation after the eruption.

**C.** Minoan culture was not wiped out by natural disaster overnight. However, if the Minoan palatial system was weakened by the eruption, it may have been susceptible to a Mycenaean takeover.

**II.** The End of the Bronze Age on the Mainland.

   **A.** A common explanation for the sudden collapse of the Mycenaean world shortly after 1200 B.C. is an invasion by the Dorians from the northwestern part of Greece.

   **1.** This theory is supported by the distribution of the Greek dialects.

   **2.** Greek myth recalled a population movement into the Peloponnese, the "Return of the Heraclidae."

   **B.** There are, however, strong arguments against the Dorian Invasion.

   **1.** Linguists doubt that the distribution of the Greek dialects in classical times is a reliable guide to population movements during a much earlier period.

   **2.** The material evidence for a Dorian invasion is poor.

   **3.** Only one segment of the Dorian population claimed to be the descendents of Heracles.

   **C.** Internal breakdown.

   **1.** A more recent explanation claims that the Dorians were already present as serfs. Linguists point to Dorian elements already to be found in the Greek of Linear B.

   **2.** The Dorian "Invasion," then, is not an external invasion, but the internal collapse of the Mycenaean social order. In this view, the Dorian servile element in Mycenaean society arose and overthrew the warrior élite.

   **D.** The theory of an internal collapse is attractive, and it fits with an historical explanation of the Trojan War.

   **1.** Greek tradition recalled a massive campaign mounted by the Achaians (the Greeks) against the wealthy city of Troy.

   **2.** The strategic position of Troy at the mouth of the Dardanelles would make sense of a campaign to capture it.

   **3.** Archaeology has demonstrated successive destruction levels at Troy, one of which (Troy VI) would be consistent with a siege.

4. Greek tradition also recalled that few of the Achaian princes returned safely to their kingdoms.
5. If the myth has a historical kernel, it may recall an expensive campaign that left the Mycenaean homeland weakened and subject to a wave of revolts.

**III.** The Sea Peoples.

    **A.** The collapse of the Mycenaean world corresponds to the widespread breakdown of civilizations throughout the eastern Mediterranean.

        **1.** The Amarna Tablets (Egypt) speak of invasions by the Sea Peoples c. 1225–1215, and they recall a time of upheaval.

        **2.** The collapse of the Hittite empire in Asia Minor occurs at about the same time.

        **3.** The Amarna Tablets mention tribes known as the Ekwesh and Akewasha, as well as the Denyen, names that seem to echo Homer's names for the Greeks: Achaians and Danaans.

    **B.** Many Mycenaeans may have left Greece during this period of turmoil and joined marauding bands to attack parts of Anatolia and Egypt.

        **1.** The Greek dialect of ancient Cyprus was closest to the Greek spoken in Arcadia, in the heart of the Peloponnese. This curious connection would make sense if Mycenaean Greeks had settled on Cyprus.

        **2.** One of the Sea Peoples, the Peleset, settled southeast of Cyprus. The Bible knows them as the Philistines, and they gave their name to the region of Palestine. The pottery found at the earliest levels of the Philistine cities is Mycenaean.

**Suggested Reading**

Wood, M. (1985) *In Search of the Trojan War.* London.

**Questions to Consider**

1. How reliable are the Homeric poems as a guide to the world of the Bronze Aegean?

**2.** Should the collapse of Myceneaen power be explained by internal factors or is it part of an historical movement affecting the entire eastern Mediterranean?

# Lecture Four—Transcript
## The Long Twilight

Welcome back to our series of lectures on Ancient Greek Civilization. In this the fourth lecture, we're going to look once again at the end of the Bronze Age. You'll remember that in our last lecture, I was making a point that we probably know more about the end of the Bronze Age than the Greeks did themselves. I was trying to emphasize the importance of this to the Greeks, in that it released them, as it were, from the dead hand of the past to use their memories, myths and poems to create not a Bronze Age, but rather a Golden Age.

We'll talk a little bit more about the importance of epic poetry, particularly in the creation of this heroic memory of the past, later on, but before we proceed any further, we have to deal with some nuts and bolts. Quite simply, what happened at the end of the Bronze Age? How is it that there is such a dramatic difference between the cultures of the Bronze Age in Crete and on the mainland, and then the subsequent Iron Age cultures of Greece leading into the Archaic and eventually the Classical period?

There was, quite simply, a massive destruction. There was a dramatic end to the Bronze Age, but the reasons and causes for this and the exact nature of this catastrophe at the end of the Bronze Age remain one of the most vexed issues in Greek archaeology. It's excited debate now for at least 100 years.

What I want to do for much of the lecture today is to talk about some of the theories that are being offered for the end of Bronze Age culture and the collapse of the Bronze Age in Greece. By far, the most dramatic explanation that has ever been offered, and one that remains romantically powerful in people's imaginations, is the notion that the Bronze Age ended because of volcanic destruction. This in particular can be used to explain the collapse of Cretan power, it is often supposed. We have to admit that the evidence here is powerful and it is in some respects quite overwhelming—quite literally in the case of the island of Thera.

If you sail today into the island of Thera, you will find that your boat will not pull up at a beach, jetty or port as in any other island of the Aegean or the Mediterranean. In fact, what you will be sailing into is the caldera (the "cauldron") of an exploded volcano. Thera lies about

200 miles northeast of Crete. It was clearly wiped out in one single massive volcanic eruption and it is sometimes been suggested that this eruption not only wiped out Thera, but also wiped out Cretan culture as well.

The story of the finding of Thera is in itself fascinating. The story here really depends upon the construction of the Suez Canal. The Suez Canal required for its construction hydraulic cement, and hydraulic cement requires for its manufacturing a certain type of volcanic stone. One source of this is in southern Italy and another source was the island of Thera. It was in the process of literally skimming off foot after foot of this volcanic ash and stone that engineers came down on top of a Bronze Age town that had been buried thousands of years ago. It was an extraordinarily dramatic discovery. It was that overburden of material that had blown up from the volcano and rained down, burying the town of Thera, that led people to suggest that this dramatic explosion had wiped out not only this Cretan colony (or Cretan-influenced town) in the Aegean, but that its effects had been felt down on Crete itself.

For example, Spiridon Marinatos, a very fine Greek excavator of early this century, pointed to a site on the northern coast of Crete at Tylissos, where he was able to show large orthostatic stones that had been sucked out of position and pulled back again in the other direction. He said this was due to the effects of a huge tidal wave generated by the volcanic eruption that lacerated the coast of Crete and then sucked people, goods and property back out to sea as it left, unfortunately, in a way that we know can happen from events this last summer, when a tsunami hit the north coast of New Guinea. Villages there were wiped out by exactly such a dramatic action.

We have this volcanic evidence from Thera. We have what might have been evidence of its effect on Crete itself supporting this. Then there is a third piece of evidence that is sometimes induced to support this very dramatic explanation for the collapse of Minoan Crete. Once again, we go back to the realm of Greek mythology. We have already talked about Theseus and the Minotaur as possibly a folk memory and myth based on the idea of a Mycenaean invasion overthrowing Minoan power. There are other stories in Greek myth about the dramatic cataclysmic end of a great civilization. I'm referring, of course, to the stories of Atlantis found in Plato's *Critias* and *Timaeus*.

These stories written down by Plato early in the fourth century B.C. are obviously written long after the volcanic explosion and long after the Bronze Age, but many people have suggested they have within them the kernel—the seed—of an actual memory of some extraordinary cataclysm. You remember that according to Plato, this wonderful society of Atlantis was wiped out suddenly and sank into the ocean. It's very tempting to try to make both the archaeology and the myth correspond in ways that we've already been doing in the last couple of lectures.

Although the volcanic theory is extremely romantic and very attractive, it's wrong. There are a number of very solid reasons for dismissing it as the primary explanation for the collapse of Minoan power on Crete. The first is that in recent years, our scientific understanding of the eruption that took place at Thera has increased enormously. We've been able to use core samples, taken from the Arctic Circle and from the floor of the Mediterranean, and tree ring evidence from all these areas to give a much more reliable date to the eruption of Thera. The eruption took place close to 1600 B.C. As we know, the palaces on Crete were still quite happily functioning in 1600 B.C. and continued to do so down at least until 1450 B.C., or 150 years later.

It is simply incorrect to suppose that when Thera blew up overnight, or even very soon after, Cretan civilization came to an abrupt end. It didn't.

This scientific evidence corroborates some pottery evidence which has been traditionally used to try to understand the relationship between Thera and Crete more closely. We know that both on Crete and on Thera, the same types of pottery were being used. However, on Minoan Crete one of the last forms of pottery that we get is known as "marine style." Marine style pottery, of course, has on it motifs borrowed from the sea, the place where the Minoans were trading. They put squid, dolphins and so forth on their vessels. This type of pottery is not found on Thera and we have to explain that gap. The most logical explanation is that Thera blew up and after it blew up, the Cretans back on Crete devised their marine style pottery. That would be concrete evidence in the pottery record that Crete was not wiped out by the Theran explosion and rather continued to exist for some time afterwards.

There is a third body of evidence, and I'm very pleased to say this is quite current archaeological evidence of the last 10 years or so. Excavations by Temple University and the University of Pennsylvania at sites on the coast of northeastern Crete at Pseira and Mochlos have brought to light the ash layer that we associate with that great cloud of ash coming from Thera. What we find "on" that ash layer—that is to say, after it's been deposited—is fresh building. In other words, the people in northeastern Crete, who were closest to Thera (200 miles away from it), were not so completely overwhelmed that they were killed outright, as, for example, were the people of Pompeii and Herculaneum. Rather, they lived long enough to go back, clean up their houses and then build new ones on top of the debris left by this Theran explosion.

I think we can fairly emphatically say that the explosion, though a romantic story, will not explain the collapse of Cretan power. It may have weakened the Cretans in some respects. For example, if we regard Thera as being a Minoan outpost, colony or trading emporium, it may have been that a Minoan fleet was wiped out in this explosion, but we really cannot give any detailed answer to this. We don't know exactly its impact.

Instead, the solution that I was trying to impose in the last lecture was something that really extends over a longer period: not a dramatic collapse of Minoan power at one moment, but rather something more along the lines of a subtle shift of power. In 1600 B.C., the Minoans are powerful, but by 1400 B.C., their influence has been taken over by the Mycenaeans. That would mean that we would be dealing with something like conflict between the two cultures out in the sphere of influence of the two cultures—their trading area of the Aegean and the eastern Mediterranean.

It's very interesting to note that at Thera, where we still have frescoes and wall paintings preserved, we see examples of paintings that show large naval expeditions heading off from an island, and we see in other registers of these same frescoes and wall paintings soldiers disembarking and charging onto land. I think that it's in the islands that the war is going on between Minoan Crete and Mycenaean Greece. It's there that the balance of power shifts. It is as a result of that that Minoan Crete, irreparably weakened and less able to control trade in the Mediterranean, is eventually subject to invasion from the mainland. Of course, the evidence supporting this, then, is to be found in Linear B, the tablets that are found in Knossos in its last phase of existence and are also found on the mainland at the Mycenaean sites.

Unfortunately, I can't give you a dramatic explanation for the end of Minoan Crete. Instead, I'm giving you one that sees a shift from Minoan to Mycenaean power.

But Mycenaean power also vanished and here it did vanish somewhat more abruptly, shortly after 1200 B.C. The question I want to pose is not what happened to the Minoans—I think we can answer that—but what happened to the Mycenaeans, the second of the great Bronze Age cultures? Why did it collapse? What happened to their power and their magnificent authority as we see in the bastions of Mycenae?

There are a couple theories that have been advanced to explain the sudden collapse of Mycenaean power and now we should take a look at those. In the early part of this century and certainly throughout the 19th century, in many textbooks the most common explanation was that the Mycenaean Greeks had been defeated and militarily overwhelmed by the Dorians. Who are the Dorians? The Dorians are Greeks, too. They're Greeks, however, not from the Mycenaean realm of central and southern Greece, but they're Greeks of the far northern part of Greece, the area now called Epirus and into Albania.

According to this theory, which was extremely popular with German historians in the last century, but, as I say, is still widely supported by many people, the Dorians had come into Greece around 1900 with the other Greek speakers. While Mycenaean power had been growing in southern Greece, they had remained apart—a separate people in the North. Then, towards the end of the Bronze Age, around 1200–1100 B.C., these Dorians came pouring out of the North and quite simply physically overwhelmed their Mycenaean cousins to the South.

What are the merits to this theory? What's it got in support of it? One of the interesting things that it does have in support of it is the distribution of the Greek dialects. Greeks speak different types of Greek in different parts of Greece, just as there are different accents and intonations in different parts of America or in Britain. The families of the Greek dialects can be largely grouped into a western Greek and eastern Greek.

The distribution of these, particularly of western Greek from the northwest down into the Peloponnese, and of eastern Greek from Attica, where Athens is located, and across the sea to the islands, has been taken as evidence by some for population movement. Greek speakers from the northwest pour in and take over the Peloponnese, so their language is found both in the Peloponnese and in the north. The east Greek speakers are pushed out and dispossessed, so you only find a pocket of their language in Athens and the rest of their language spoken further out in the islands. That's an attractive theory.

Another bit of evidence that may support this idea of the Dorian invasions is a Greek myth. Once again I'll call upon the Greeks themselves. That is the story of the "Return of the Heraclidae." The Heraclidae are the sons of Heracles and they're to be found in the Peloponnese. The people living in the Peloponnese who claimed to be the sons and descendents of Heracles maintained that they had once had power in the Peloponnese. They had been briefly dispossessed, but now they had returned. Again, you can see that a myth that talks about a population movement coming into the Peloponnese could be used to support the notion of an actual invasion by Dorians.

I still don't like it, though. You can probably tell by the way I'm summarizing the argument that I'm not going to support it. Let me give you the reasons why I think the Dorian invasion is not a good explanation for the end of the Mycenaean world. In the first place, linguists believe that the distribution of the Greek dialect is not a reliable guide to the population movements which occurred so much earlier. Some go on and point out that it would be very difficult to explain the presence of the Dorians for 400 or 500 years as Greek speakers sufficiently intelligible to the southern Greeks, but somehow outside the Mycenaean world at the same time. Linguistically, it's not entirely clear that you can use a map and say these people speak this dialect, therefore they came from this place.

Probably more compelling, though, is this problem. There's no material evidence for the Dorians. If you ask, "What is the culture of the Dorians?," it used to be that historians would point to a certain type of pottery, until it was found that Dorian pottery was usually found in places that weren't Dorian, like Athens, and they were found there supposedly before the Dorians were there. There is no material culture that we can tie to the Dorians, so that makes the idea of a Dorian invasion somewhat difficult.

As for the story of the sons of Heracles, it is true that some people in the Peloponnese claim to have been descended from Heracles and to have come back to the Peloponnese, but the Greeks were very clear that claiming that you were Dorian and claiming that you were of the sons of Heracles were not the same claim at all.

In recent years, worried by these gaps and holes in the theory of a Dorian invasion, some historians have gone back to the evidence and postulated a new theory, one which I like very much: that is that the Dorians were there all along. They were in the Mycenaean world. They were part of the Mycenaean world. In support of this, there is linguistic evidence. Some say that linguistically, there are Dorian elements that you can find in Linear B Greek.

What on earth would it mean if you were to say the Dorians were there all along? What it would mean is that this could be the servile population, not the elite. Not the Agamemnons, Menelauses, and great heroes of the Achaians, Greeks and Mycenaeans, but rather the Dorians were the workers, farmers and serfs who, for whatever reason, in fact overthrew their Mycenaean overlords. According to this theory, the Dorian invasion would not, in fact, be an inversion from outside Mycenaean Greece; it would be an internal upheaval, sometimes grandly called a "systems collapse."

Is there any further evidence that we can bring to bear on this argument to see? The idea of an internal collapse is an interesting one, particularly if you posit a Mycenaean world which, around 1200 B.C., had become immensely fragile, one in which the social order that maintained the power of this warrior elite was somehow under threat. Can we imagine a set of circumstances where for one reason or another, the world of these Mycenaean princes might have been threatened to such a degree that their Dorian slaves and serfs might rise up and expel their Mycenaean overlords?

Here we get to the favorite topic of every Greek archaeologist and pre-historian, the Trojan War. If there is historical truth in the story of the Trojan War, I think it bears on this problem right now. Let's rehearse some of the details here and see if we can make sense out of this. Greek tradition in later years maintained definitely that there had been a massive campaign mounted by dozens of powerful princes, who had led an armada to the Troad, up near the Hellespont (the Dardanelles), where there is a passage by sea up to the Black Sea.

In this tradition, the Greeks, who Homer calls the Achaians, go and lay siege to the city for 10 years. As we know from talking about Schliemann, he excavated at Troy using Homer as his guide and there is a site there which continued to be occupied in antiquity even into classical times, which people thought of as being the site of historical Troy. When Schliemann excavated it, he found a brilliant Bronze Age civilization. In fact, he found many Bronze Age civilizations in that one spot. There are layers of them, one on top of each other.

The position of Troy—of Schliemann's Troy, of Homer's Troy—makes good sense. It is strategically very important. Why? For a very simple reason: if you want to get from the Aegean to the Black Sea and you must go up the Dardanelles, the current—the water flowing out of the Black Sea—is bringing you down. It is preventing you from sailing up. The only way that you can get up the Dardanelles, then, is if you have a wind behind you taking you up. If the wind turns while you're on your way up, then you have to pull into port very quickly. You need protection, because the current will take you straight back out into the Aegean.

Troy is strategically well-situated to control the sea-born trade traveling between the Black Sea and the Aegean.

We have a site and we have a memory of a war being fought there. What do we have archaeologically? We have many different Troys, as I've said. They're layered upon layered upon layered. It seems to be that of the various levels of Troy that have been excavated, the Troys which are called "Troy VI," "Troy VII-A" and "Troy VII-B" correspond, generally speaking, to the end of the Bronze Age. What we've got at the end of the Bronze Age at Troy is a major citadel with extremely well-built walls reinforced by towers with terraces leading up to the top of the hill, upon which would have been the king's palace or megaron. It was subsequently torn away by later building, but it would have been there.

We've got a Troy of the right period. Now, let's ask, "Do we have a destruction of the right period?" Can we point to Troy VI or VII and say, "Here we have definitive evidence for a Troy being destroyed by an army of occupation laying siege to it." As everything in archaeology goes, the answer is yes and no. The answer is yes, we do have destruction levels, but I put it to you: when an archaeologist talks about a "destruction level," what he or she is talking about is a nice thick layer of black ash that shows you that everything burnt. It's very difficult to say definitively that such a layer is created by an army which has laid siege to a site and burnt it, or whether a site suffered an earthquake, caught fire and burnt down.

We have suggestive archaeological evidence which would allow us to imagine one of the Bronze Age Troys being destroyed by warfare and attack. Putting these together, what do we end up with? It's a bit of a stretch, I'll agree, but bear with me. The way I would put it together is like this: in Homer's myth of the Trojan War, we have a memory that has undergone change over the course of centuries as oral poetry tells the story again and again. The historical kernel of that story is that late in the Bronze Age, Mycenaean Greeks mounted a massive campaign against Troy. Whether they were actually successful or not, I don't know. Whether they built a Trojan horse, which was then taken inside the walls, I doubt, but I won't commit myself to it.

But I want to point out one other feature of the historical tradition and the poetic tradition which I think is worth keeping in mind. That is that in addition to the epic poems that dealt with the sack of Troy, the Greeks had another cycle of epic poems called "The Nostoi," and these are the returns of the great heroes from Troy. Think for a moment what befell the various heroes. Ajax committed suicide. Agamemnon, the king of men and ships, returned to Mycenae to be stabbed in his bath by his adulterous wife and her lover. Odysseus, spent 10 years at war and 10 years frantically trying to get back home again to find his family grown up and almost unrecognizable and much of his property and goods eaten by the suitors.

The overwhelming tradition of the Greeks about these returns was that they had been disastrous. In that, I like to think we have a memory of a campaign to Troy which proved to be overwhelmingly disastrous to the Mycenaean world, weakening the Mycenaean kingdoms and eventually seeing the power of Mycenae overwhelmed by not a Dorian invasion, but a Dorian explosion.

Finally, I want to try to put this into a little perspective. We've been concentrating exclusively on the Bronze Age in the Greek world.

We've talked about Crete and Mycenae. We've talked about the collapse of these cultures purely in terms of Crete, Mycenae and perhaps Troy. In fact, the collapse of the Bronze Age was not merely a Greek phenomenon. It occurred in the 12th and 11th century B.C. around the entire eastern Mediterranean. For example, we have Egyptian records that speak at this time of Ramses winning victories over people who had been attacking the Delta—the so-called Sea Peoples. It looks as if somebody's pouring into Egypt at the same time. We know of the collapse of Hittite power. The great Hittite empire of Anatolia, with its capital Hattusas at modern Bogazköy, simply ceases to exist around 1215 B.C.

We have a number of upheavals in the late Bronze Age and I think we can position the Mycenaeans in this upheaval a little more precisely. It's this way: the Sea Peoples recorded in the Egyptian records include some very suggestive names, names that often suggest where people later ended up in history. The Shardana, for example, are probably those who end up in Sardinia, and the Tyrshenoi probably end up in Tuscany—Etruria, the Etruscans.

Among the various tribes mentioned among the Sea Peoples are the Ekwesh and the Denyen. These names appear to be Egyptian versions or renderings, if you will, of the names which we would recognize in Greek as *Achaioi* and *Danaoi*—the Achaians and the Danaans as we would call them in English.

These are the names by which Homer refers to the Greeks, and yet they're turning up amongst the lists of the Sea Peoples. What's happened? I think we've got records here of Mycenaean Greeks abandoning Greece—leaving Greece and sailing off elsewhere. The Mycenaean Greeks are then both part of the collapse of Bronze Age civilization and part of the cause of it. They suffer its effects and they also contribute to it.

Let me finish with two last bits of evidence. Do we have any evidence that might lead us to think that the Mycenaeans abandoned Greece—they abandoned their sites, no longer able to control those populations who had been enthralled to them earlier? One bit of evidence is that the language spoken on Cyprus was a dialect of Greek that is also found in the central Peloponnese: Arcado-Cypriot. That linguistic similarity would make sense if people from the Peloponnese got in their boats and sailed off to Cyprus. That's one possibility.

The other is this: among the Sea Peoples are a group called the Peleset. You might be able to guess what place or region they give their name to. The place of the Peleset is Palestine. They're also known in other records, in the Bible for example, as the "Philistines"—the Peleset, the Philistines, Palestine.

Here's an interesting thought: when you excavate to the bottom earliest layers of the cities occupied by the Philistines, the type of pottery that you find there is Mycenaean. I suggest to you that one possible explanation is that the Peleset include in their ranks Mycenaean Greeks—that some people never returned from Troy. Whether it was specifically a 10-year war and whether they specifically sacked Troy, I don't know. But I think we have enough to believe in a Trojan War of sorts, a cataclysmic event that weakened Greece, and that the rulers of the Mycenaean kingdoms of Greece either returned to find themselves under attack or never returned at all.

I kind of like the idea, I guess to pull this all together, that Goliath of Gath may have been the grandson of Agamemnon.

# Lecture Five
# The Age of Heroes

**Scope:**

With the passing of the Bronze Age between 1200 and 1100 B.C., Greek culture underwent profound changes. Central authority collapsed, to be replaced in most areas by the more humble power of chieftains and clan leaders. The society that emerged during these so-called Dark Ages was organized around neither the palace nor the fortress, but around the *oikos* or household. This would become the principal social unit of the Greeks, and it would underpin the rise of the *polis* or city-state.

All was not chaos and destruction, however. In the last generation, archaeology has supplied surprising evidence of a more rapid recovery than was previously suspected. This was a critical period for the Greeks in another respect, since it was at this time that epic poetry arose. The Greeks would return to the *Iliad* and the *Odyssey* endlessly. Their codes of honor, their notions of the relation between god and human, man and woman, parent and child—in short, their entire mentality—was conditioned by the imaginative world created by Homer and the epic tradition.

## Outline

**I.** The World of the *Oikos.*

    **A.** The evidence of material culture suggests a serious decline in the number and the size of settlements throughout Greece in the period from 1200–900 B.C.

    **B.** Population decline is not the only, or even the best, answer. Instead it seems that many people had resumed herding in the hills in order to escape the dangers of an unsettled time.

    **C.** Many of the massive Mycenaean fortified sites were either totally abandoned or occupied by squatters.

    **D.** Replacing the Bronze Age world was a new type of society, structured around smaller social units dominated by chieftains and clan leaders. The household, known as the *oikos*, was the central unit of Dark-Age society.

**II.** Signs of Recovery.

    **A.** Despite the grim picture of Greece after the Mycenaeans, recent archaeology has demonstrated that in some places recovery came faster than expected.

        **1.** At Lefkandi, a monumental apsidal building dating to the tenth century was used as a massive funerary structure for a royal pair.

        **2.** At Elateia, tombs excavated during the 1990s reveal a community already producing fine pottery and metal work, and engaged in trade that went beyond Greece.

        **3.** At Kalapodi, a sanctuary that goes back to Mycenaean times continued in use down into the Sub-Mycenaean period and throughout the Dark Ages.

    **B.** It is probably no coincidence that these sites are close together in central and eastern Greece. They lie on the outer edges of the Mycenaean world. The worst collapse had been in the Peloponnese, the Mycenaean heartland, but recovery began on the periphery.

    **C.** It is hard to find explicit continuities between the Bronze Age and the Dark and Iron Ages in Greece.

        **1.** Greeks in both periods spoke Greek, but their writing systems were completely different.

        **2.** Certain gods and goddesses appear in both Mycenaean and classical records, but other classical-era gods have no Mycenaean roots.

        **3.** Certain locations remain sacred over time, even though the religious systems that endow the spot with sacred meaning might change.

        **4.** Bronze Age royal palaces often became classical-era temples, evidencing continuity of a sort.

**III.** Epic and the *Polis.*

    **A.** Aside from the material recovery that occurred during the Dark Ages, another crucial development took place: the rise of epic poetry.

        **1.** Epic consisted of cycles of songs concerning the deeds of great warriors.

        **2.** The songs were highly formulaic, allowing some sections to be reused and newer parts to be composed orally.

3. Wandering poets performed these songs all over Greece, incorporating the accomplishments of local heroes.
4. The greatest of the poems, the *Iliad* and the *Odyssey*, were written down around 725 B.C. The previously flexible oral tradition thus became solidified in a single, monumental version.
5. By then, the poems had created a consistent legendary world that connected the Greeks to a heroic past, centered on the Trojan War and the return of the heroes.
6. The importance of the poems is that they nurtured a sense of Greek identity even as the Greeks remained politically fragmented.
   a. The poems upheld a heroic code of behavior for superior men, as illustrated by the exchange between the Trojan heroes Sarpedon and Glaucus.
   b. They also link heroism with steadfast adherence to duty in the face of overwhelming odds, as shown by Hector's response to Andromache.

B. From the eighth century on, the political development of the Greeks was focused on the city-state (*polis*) and the tribal-state (*ethnos*).
1. These states emphasized their own autonomy and separateness.
2. The Greeks showed no interest in founding a Greek nation. They were united only in times of crisis.
3. By providing a powerful statement of Greek values, epics made possible the central paradox of ancient Greek culture: being Greek meant being like other Greeks in cultural terms while remaining completely distinct from other Greeks in political terms.

## Suggested Reading

Desborough, V.R. d'A. (1964) *The Last Mycenaeans and Their Successors, An Archaeological Survey, c. 1200-c.1000 B.C.* Oxford: Clarendon Press.

_____ (1972) *The Greek Dark Ages*. New York: St Martin's Press.

Snodgrass, A.M. (1971) *The Dark Age of Greece*. Edinburgh: The University Press.

**Questions to Consider**

1.  How important is a shared sense of the past to the development of a national identity?

2.  What are the values that Homer's poems reinforce?

# Lecture Five—Transcript
## The Age of Heroes

Welcome back to our series of lectures on Ancient Greek Civilization. In the last couple of lectures, we've been looking primarily at the Bronze Age. We've looked at Minoan Crete and at Mycenaean Greece. In addition to describing those cultures, we've also tried to have a look at some of the explanations for the collapse of that Bronze Age world. We've looked at various theories and I think that we can conclude by saying we're probably never going to know exactly why the Bronze Age cultures of Greece collapsed as they did—but they did. That we can be sure of.

We can be sure of that because archaeologically if you go to most of the great Bronze Age sites, you will find that their occupation history stops abruptly sometime after 1200 B.C. You'll find that if you continue around Greece looking at archaeological sites all over the country and in Crete as well, you'll find a general pattern being repeated all over the country: that is of a serious decline in the number of sites and in the size of sites as the centuries progress on from the 12<sup>th</sup> century B.C.

Let me give you an illustration. If you were to go around Greece now and look at sites that we know were occupied in the 13<sup>th</sup> century B.C., you would find about 320 of them. If you were then to ask how many sites do we have in the same area that were occupied 100 years later, the number has shrunk from 320 down to about 130. If you go along then another 100 years after that, the number shrinks even further to 40. Not only do the numbers shrink, but if we can judge the size of the settlement by the size of the burial population that we have in cemeteries around Greece, that also is shrinking. There are fewer people.

There are various ways of explaining these rather startling figures. One is that there's a change in the places where people live. They're literally hightailing it for the hills. I want to give you a little illustration of that from my own experience from excavating about 10 years ago in Crete. In the eastern side of Crete, there is a site called La Vronda. It is a middle Minoan site—it dates from the middle towards the end of the second millennium B.C. Then the occupation history at the site stops.

If you climb up the mountains, and I did this every day for many months, and climb right to the top of the mountain behind it (it's called Kastro) and excavate up there, you'll find that there is a site which we know was occupied in the geometric period in the early Iron Age. We wanted to know what the connection was between the two. The hypothesis was that at the end of Minoan times in the Bronze Age, life became critical, there were marauders and pirates, and there was a breakdown of social order. One of the ways people dealt with this was by escaping from their vulnerable area down in the plain and going up to the hills where they could hide on the mountaintops.

We excavated there for a number of years and finally, during one of the seasons, we came right down to the bottom layer. I know it's the bottom, because below it was bedrock. At the bottom layer in four separate squares on the Kastro, we found late Minoan pottery, exactly the level you would expect if people had abandoned their middle Minoan site and then gone up into the hills.

As you go around Crete, for example, you can visit sites such as Karfi, located in central Crete, where you will see that people went up hundreds of meters to escape from the plain. It's a wonderful site in terms of the vision that you get with the Mediterranean in front of you, but you have to be a goat to get up there. These people were hiding—getting away from a society that was collapsing and in crisis.

If you've looked at the mainland, you've seen many of these great Mycenaean fortresses and the walls of Mycenae and looked at places like Tiryns, Gla and Orchomenos. What we find is that after about 1200 B.C., there is no central authority any longer. Walls begin to collapse. Places are either totally abandoned or, in some cases, we can attest to squatters. That is to say, we can see small rubble walls being put up in the shadow of the great Cyclopean masonry that had existed there for hundreds of years before them.

We've got a great change going on in terms of the quality of life. We have a real downturn, if you like, at the end of the Bronze Age. Those population figures that I gave you earlier, though, are interesting because many demographers have looked at this and said, "You know, if a population declined that drastically over that short a space of time, it actually could not sustain itself. They would have all died out."

We have to try to interpret that evidence in a slightly different way. One of the ways I would suggest is that many of the people who used to live at these Mycenaean sites—let's say the workmen, perfume makers, and shield makers who lived in the suburbs below the citadel at Mycenae, for example—when central authority breaks down and nobody can pay the bills or supply them with the food they need, they don't just starve. What they do is they run away and become herdsmen. They take their flocks. Shepherds, less commonly cowherds, and very commonly goatherds take to the hills.

If you think about it for a moment, you might be able to see why it is that it's so hard to trace them archaeologically. I thought of this once when driving towards Mount Parnassus. I pulled over and saw a Greek shepherd by the road who'd been on the road for months. At the end of the day, he was building a small lean-to made out of wattle and daub—out of bushes and branches that he'd cut and put together.

I tried to imagine what his ancestors would have been like thousands of years ago and it occurred to me that you're talking about a man wearing animal skins with a flock of goats and a bowl made of wood for milking these animals, which he perhaps wears around his neck on a leather strap during the day. He lives at night in a lean-to made of thatch. Ask yourself this: 100 years after that man is dead and gone, what is the archaeological trace that he's left? The answer is zero—absolutely nothing.

The life of the itinerant herder moving his herds from pasture to pasture across the hills and up into the mountains and down into the plain is a type of lifestyle that makes sense during times of crisis. You are mobile. But it leaves very little record for the archaeologists and it's very hard to track down later on.

Replacing the Bronze Age world, this brilliant culture that we've been looking at, a new type of society would soon emerge during the Dark Ages, the period from about 1100–800 B.C. This is a world which would be dominated not by the great kings of the Mycenaean palaces, but rather by chieftains. They would still go by the same name. They'd be called *basileus* in the plural.

Their domains, rather than that of a great Mycenaean kingdom, would be rather smaller. It would be a domain centered on a single household. The technical term for this in Greek is the *oikos*. This *oikos* is the central social unit of the Dark Ages in Greece. It's in a single long hut, where a chieftain would have his wife, perhaps his aged parents and children, his retainers, people who'd attached themselves to his household for their protection, his serfs, his slaves, and his property, including his goats and sheep occasionally being brought in. This is the unit of life that dominates in the Dark Ages. It is materially not nearly as sophisticated, of course, as the much more complex social life of the Bronze Age at Mycenae or Minoan Crete.

Nevertheless, there's been a tendency in classical studies in archaeology to overemphasize the grimness of this break—to suggest that the world after the Mycenaeans was one that was quite literally dark for 300 years, where nobody had any lamps, and the level of poverty was so grinding that the Greeks only very slowly clawed their way back to a full culture. That picture is very easily overdrawn. It's somewhat exaggerated.

There is evidence, and here again I rehearse evidence that's really from the last generation and in particular from the last 10 years, to suggest that the level of recovery was much greater and much faster in some parts of Greece than has ever been previously expected.

There are three places in particular that have made archaeologists rethink what they sometimes call the "Sub-Mycenaean period" (the 10th and ninth centuries B.C., the Dark Ages). At Lefkandi, for example, on the island of Euboea, we have a monumental building— an apsidal building, that is to say a long building that has a rounded end and post holes all along the side. It was built in the 10th century B.C., sometime around 950 B.C. It's quite a breathtaking structure. It's not really like anything Mycenaean, so it's something new and something different. Its scale, both of the building and of the burial goods left at Lefkandi, suggests that even as early as 950 B.C., people from Euboea were once again trading outside of Greece more widely.

Lefkandi is a very interesting place for another reason and that is that in the middle of the building, archaeologists found a burial. When they went into the middle of the building and they found this burial pit inside, they found the cremated remains of a man (that is to say that his body had been cremated, but there was enough left of the bones to determine that it was a man) and the burial of a woman and four horses. Some scholars have pointed to this as an example of what they would call a "heroic burial." In other words, this looks very much like a powerful chieftain who in death was honored by his followers and supporters perhaps by the slaughter of his wife over his tomb and the slaughtering of his four great steeds as well.

Given the fact that there are descriptions of something similar in Homer—if you think of the burial of Patroclus, for example, where horses are cremated—we may have here as early as 950 B.C. an example of a heroic behavior in which great men are really thinking of presenting themselves in the style of Homeric heroes.

Nearby, also in central Greece (on the mainland, not on the island of Euboea), at Elateia, during the 1990s a joint Austrian-Greek excavation has been excavating dozens of tombs from the Sub-Mycenaean period (from the $10^{th}$ century B.C.). They're producing there very fine pottery, they're demonstrating that people here are working once again in metalwork with precious metals, and that goods are being traded not just locally, but outside of Greece as well.

The third place that I want to mention in this brief survey of the recovery, if you will, is again located nearby in central Greece, not far from Elateia, at a sanctuary called Kalapodi. Here, a German team during the 1970s and 1980s excavated a sanctuary which had been in use not only in classical, archaic, and geometric times, but also right back continuously into the Bronze Age—into Mycenaean times.

Can we pull this information together? Can we say anything more about the Mycenaean world and what follows after it as we consider this data? I think we can. I think it's not a coincidence that the places that I've mentioned to you—Lefkandi, Elateia, and Kalapodi—all lie outside of the very central heartland of the Mycenaean world, which is to say the Peloponnese. The Argive Plain, Argos, Mycenae, Tiryns—these are the great Mycenaean citadels.

The area that we're talking about here of central Greece is not exactly a backwater, but I think it is somewhat peripheral to the center of the Mycenaean world. I suggest to you that with thought in the past about the end of the Bronze Age as being so completely catastrophic in the Mycenaean world, and because we've concentrated on those great sites in the Peloponnese, if we turn our attention a little bit further away from the Peloponnese, what we find is a different story: a less overwhelming collapse and perhaps in some way a continuity from the Bronze Age into the Dark Ages and then the Iron Age.

Continuity: I've avoided using that term so far, but I can't avoid it any further. It is the Holy Grail of Greek archaeologists. What it means is this: can you demonstrate in any given place a practice, habit, building, or style—anything at all—which is found both in the Bronze Age and is carried through into the Iron Age. Is there anything to show demonstrably that classical Greece still had and was aware of concrete, real roots in the Bronze Age?

Continuity is a tough one. It's very hard to pin this down. Let me explain a little bit why. Let's say you were to take the topic of language. We know from Linear B that those Mycenaean Greeks spoke Greek. We know from the alphabet later that the Greeks of the classical period spoke Greek. That's continuity, if you will. But of course, the writing systems of Linear B and the alphabet are utterly different. The very practice of writing was lost for at least 300 years. In that area, you have both continuity and complete separation of the two cultures, if you will.

You can think of it in other terms. What about religion? We know that there are various gods and goddesses of the classical Greeks, such as Athena and Poseidon, who occur back in Mycenaean records ("*Athana*" and "*Poseidaonwa*," as they're called). Does that mean that we have religious continuity from the Bronze Age into the classical period? In a way it does, but then we have other gods and goddesses, like Aphrodite, who seem to come in later and from outside of Greece. They're not Mycenaean at all.

To think about continuity of religion in another way, again I want to give you a little anecdote involving Greece. There is a site in central Greece called *Pigas Cephisou*, which means the "springs of the Cephisos River." Like many water sources in Greece and other parts of the world, it was considered sacred. Cephisos, the river, was also a god, so the springs of the Cephisos became a holy spot. We know that because if you go to the springs today, you can still see, cut out of the living rock, the benches on which priests sat when they officiated at ceremonies right there at the sacred pool.

Right behind them was a terrace. On the terrace was built a temple. We have dedicatory inscriptions. We know it was a temple to the god Cephisos. It doesn't stand anymore, because we only have the terrace. If you go 50 meters away from that terrace, you'll find an early Christian church, the Church of Ayia Eliuso, an early Byzantine church. It is in such a state of disrepair now that you can walk around and even look inside the walls. What you'll find nine times out of 10 is that a stone that was used for the Christian church is in fact a stone from the pagan temple reused. On one side there will be a Christian cross carved, but then turn it around on the other side and you will find some classical motif.

Continuity or not? Yes. It's a sacred spot. It was a sacred spot then; it's a sacred spot now. But the religious system that makes it sacred is completely and utterly different. I don't think anyone's going to argue that the Temple of Cephisos the River God was a Christian church.

This question of continuity or change is a very vexed and difficult one. For example, you can point out that at virtually every Mycenaean site that we know, there will be later a classical town. Where the Mycenaean palace stood, there will be later an acropolis. If you go to the Acropolis in Athens, there was a Mycenaean palace there. What was originally a Mycenaean palace and administrative center usually changes its nature and function. What was the king's palace becomes in the classical period a temple.

In the relationship between the Bronze Age and the later periods of Greek history, this question of whether culture continued or not is a very difficult one to answer. What we can say with some certainty, I think, is that the world which started to reform for the Greeks in the eighth century B.C. was going to be in most respects quite different from the Bronze Age culture that came before it. In the course of the next couple of lectures, we're going to be concentrating on the Greek world that came out of the Dark Ages in the eighth century B.C. and then in the Archaic period, down to about 500 B.C. What we're going to be seeing is a world in which the Greeks are trading much more widely. We're going to be seeing massive changes in Greece itself at Delphi and Olympia.

But I want to postpone those interesting areas for later lectures. Instead we need to concentrate on two aspects of what could be called, if you like, the "Archaic revolution"—the period, particularly the eighth century B.C., when there were fundamental changes taking place in Greece. Two of them are all we can deal with right now.

The first of them is the writing down of epic. This is a monumental step and I invite you to consider its significance for a minute. We know that during the Dark Ages, from 1100 onwards, there had been oral poets operating all over Greece. We can even say something about these oral poets' techniques now, thanks to the scholarship of Norman Parry and Alfred Lord. We know that these poets quite literally for generations were telling heroic stories, often based on some general cycle of myths such as the Trojan War or the returns of the heroes afterward.

Each of these performances would be subtly different, although sometimes not so subtly. For example, if you arrived in a small town like Thisbe and you knew that the local lord was going to be putting you up for the night, you might try and find out whether there was a hero from Thisbe involved in the Trojan War. You might work him into your presentation that night—into the poem that you're telling. Or people might tell you, "Well, we don't really know about our Homeric background, but we'd sure like to have one." Then you can manufacture a Homeric episode for that particular community.

By cobbling together both the large story of something like the Trojan War or the returns of the heroes afterwards with these local stories of heroes, what the epic poets are doing is creating something quite unique. It is a cultural document available to all the Greeks— an epic poem available for all of them.

We know that this carried on orally, as I've said, for hundreds of years all over Greece, but then something dramatic happened around 725 B.C. The dramatic shift is that somebody writes it down. When you try to consider the relationship between oral poetry—that is to say a poetry of performance that changes every time you tell a story—and a written poem, I think you'll see that they're fundamentally different. A written poem is something that you sit down and compose. An oral poem has its own genesis, if you will. In fact, writing is, if you'll pardon my expression, a kind of "arthritis" applied to oral poetry. That is to say, once you start to have written texts, the oral poem can no longer keep changing as fluidly and as often as it had been doing up until then.

It doesn't solidify completely straight away. We know that. We can look at different manuscripts and different fragments of the Homeric poems. Hundreds of years after it was first written down, we know that it was still undergoing some change, but there has certainly been a psychological shift here. A notion has been created of a single monumental version of the *Iliad* and the *Odyssey*.

What's important about that apart from the fact that we have orality moving to writing? What I think happens at this time is that the Homeric poems take on a kind of status or stature among the Greeks. They become really the nearest that the Greeks have to what we would regard as a kind of sacred text. Recall, the Greeks do not believe in a single god. They do not have a sacred text handed down from their single god, but with the writing of Homer, they do have the writing down of a moral text that they will return to time and time again.

There are many passages that you can point to in the poems that I think evoke something of this quality: the way in which the poems begin to serve as the basis for a code of moral behavior. For example, there is a point in the *Iliad* when Sarpedon and Glaucus, two of the Trojan heroes, meet on the plain of battle. In the midst of the fray, Sarpedon turns to Glaucus and he says, "Come on, we are given a double portion of wine and a double portion of meat among the Lycians, whom we rule. We have well-watered meadows by the river. We have great power among the Lycians. Now, let's go to the fore. Let's be in the first line of battle, so that any Lycians who see us will say, 'Okay, they're worth their double portion of meat and their double portion of wine. These leaders of ours, they are not slackers. They will fight.'"

In other words, the way that a Homeric hero presents himself is quite simply to be twice the size of a normal man: twice as strong, twice as powerful, and twice as steadfast.

What the poems do, by creating such a vivid model for a man's behavior, is to establish this code of honor, which is based not upon the guilt of a man ("Gee, if I do that, I'm sinning"), but rather on his shame ("If I do that, I'm going to be seen to be inferior"). The entire focus of this is to create a performance of valor, whether it be military valor or, as we're going to see soon in another lecture, athletic valor. Either way you look at it, the Homeric hero becomes the basis of what a Greek man is going to model himself on.

I may have given the impression that the poems are two dimensional, that they simply lay out how you're supposed to be. They're much more than that. To balance the anecdote of Sarpedon and Glaucus, I have to refer to another episode which is also critical in the poems. It's one of the few moments of true intimacy in the *Iliad*.

The *Iliad* is a poem of war. It tells men how to behave in war, so it has very little space for the world of the family and community. Ironically, of course, it's the enemy who represent family and community. It's the Trojans, not the Achaians, or the Greeks. In some ways, the greatest hero of the poem is not the Greek hero Achilles, who becomes virtually a maniac in his fury and drowns the river Scamander with dead bodies.

Rather, it's the Trojan hero, Hector. Throughout the poem we know that Hector's going to die. There comes a moment, I think it's in Book 6, where Hector comes back from battle. He's still wearing his helmet and he's still covered in gore. He comes in to look to see where his wife is and they tell him that she's up on the battlements. He goes up there and there is Andromache holding the little baby Astyanax. He comes up to her and when she suggests to him that maybe he should stay out of battle for awhile, he says, "Look, I know that Troy is going to fall and I know that one day, all the men here—my brothers—will be slaughtered. I know that you're going to be dragged off to Greece to be someone's slave. I only hope that when that happens, I will be dead and in the ground and people at least will say of me that I fought the best that I could."

There is no suggestion that his heroism is going to save Troy. Rather, it is that his heroism is all the greater because he knows his duty and he will stay until the bitter end. That notion, I think, was deeply imbedded in the Greeks. It took hold, so that at a later point, in Spartan history, a Spartan by the name of Kallikratidas was facing overwhelming odds on the battlefield and was told he should just get away while he could. His reply was, "If I stay and die, Sparta loses nothing. If I run away and live, both Sparta and I have been dishonored."

That is a purely Homeric sentiment, yet it was something that men were still trying to live by hundreds of years after Homer had stopped composing and the poems had been written down.

There's another aspect of this eighth century B.C. that I need to mention briefly. That is that what we're seeing at the same time that these Homeric poems are being written down, and as Greek culture is arriving at its master work so early in its history, is that there is another change going on materially. Gradually in the eighth century B.C. and then more in the seventh and the sixth B.C., but beginning in the eighth B.C., we're finding that those single households—those *oikoi* (the households of the great men that I was talking about earlier)—are getting large enough that they actually begin to coalesce. Households turn into hamlets. Hamlets turn into villages, and villages will now begin to turn into towns.

What is happening at this time is that we are seeing the first steps towards the emergence of a political community, which will be the characteristic form for the rest of Greek history: the "*polis*"—the city state. It will be an area of territory, usually with some capital at the center, with cults and temples built on its outer edges in order to proclaim that this is part of their territory. What's interesting about the Greeks is that neither these poleis (city-states) nor the ethnic confederations of northern Greece (the *ethnai* or the tribal states as they're called) proceeded any further and coalesced to become a nation.

It may seem a little anachronistic to ask why did the Greeks not proceed that far? I could be guilty of the charge of thinking in modern terms: we have nation states, why didn't they? But I think it's important to recognize how fixed the Greeks were on their separate communities. Each of these Greek states emerging in the eighth century B.C. and beyond vigorously asserts its own independence and autonomy. As a result, the Greeks show no interest in ever ending their differences and forming a larger Greek nation. They do it temporarily in times of crisis, but never on anything like a permanent basis.

I think epic is playing a role here. What I want to suggest to you over the course of the next couple of lectures is that what the Greeks had in place of a political unity was a cultural unity. There was no need for a Greek nation or a Greek state and no need for a Greek empire in the style of the Roman Empire or anything like that. There was a Greek culture. If you spoke Greek, if you had Greek blood in your veins, and if you participated in Greek institutions, you were a Greek. At the very core of that—at the very heart of what it is to be Greek—is epic and the world of Homer. Epic becomes, then, a powerful statement of Greek values.

Finally, I think it makes possible a kind of paradox that's at the center of Greek history. Being Greek meant being like the other

Greeks certainly, yet at the same time, it meant remaining completely distinct from all the other Greeks.

# Lecture Six
# From Sicily to Syria—
# The Growth of Trade and Colonization

**Scope:**

From a very early date the Greeks vigorously colonized both the Mediterranean and Black Seas. The first wave of colonization, from the mainland to the Ionian coast (the eastern seaboard of the Aegean) occurred shortly after 1000 B.C., and it reflected the upheavals occurring in the unsettled period following the end of the Mycenaean world. Then, during the seventh and sixth centuries, a fresh wave of colonization took place. This resulted in Greek colonies being established as far away as Olbia in Ukraine, and Massilia on the south coast of France.

In this lecture we consider the causes of this colonization. Did Greece suffer from massive overpopulation which was then siphoned off by dispatching unwanted sons to new lands? Did land hunger drive many Greeks to abandon a homeland where good soil was at a premium? Or did trade open new vistas to the Greeks as they searched for raw materials and markets?

We will also consider the impact on the Greeks of becoming colonists. Many of the colonies grew much richer than their "mother-city." What was the impact of this wealth on the colonies and the homeland? Colonies also had a profound influence on the Greek world, being responsible, among other things, for the introduction of writing to Greece.

## Outline

**I.** Where, When, and Why?

    **A.** The Greek colonies established during the Archaic period (c. 700-480 B.C.) where not dispatched at once but in successive waves.

    **B.** The Greeks planted their colonies wherever conditions were favorable and local resistance could be overcome. Since much of the eastern Mediterranean was unavailable, they concentrated on the Black Sea, the western Mediterranean and parts of North Africa.

**C.** Most of the colonies were founded close to the sea, not inland, invariably close to reliable sources of fresh water and large stretches of fertile land.

    **1.** By contrast, in Greece, mountains reduce the amount of fertile land in the plains to a minimum.

    **2.** Colonies were therefore a useful way of easing the hunger for good land in Greece.

    **3.** Inheritance by eldest sons encouraged younger sons to seek their fortunes overseas.

    **4.** Colonies were also a safety valve for mounting pressure and conflict (*stasis*) within many emerging city-states.

**D.** Although a single city provided the official founder of the colony, most colonies were a mixture of Greeks from different towns and regions. Foundation legends and the approval of the Delphic Oracle helped establish a common identity for the colonists.

**II.** The Role of Trade.

**A.** While land-hunger and social pressure in Greece spurred the growth of colonies, trade also played an important role. At sites such as Pithecoussae (Italy), Al Mina (Syria), and Naucratis (Egypt), Greeks traded with, and settled next to, non-Greeks, especially traders from the Phoenician cities of Tyre, Sidon, and Carthage.

**B.** Trade therefore established routes along which the Greeks sailed and helped determine where the Greeks looked to colonize.

    **1.** The Greek colonies of southern Italy and Sicily demonstrate this confluence. The earliest Greek settlements in the Bay of Naples were at the intersection of trade routes from west and north. Soon they were followed by agricultural colonies established in Sicily and southern Italy (Magna Graecia).

    **2.** In Magna Graecia the rich opportunities for trade and colonization resulted in a region of phenomenal wealth that would far outstrip old Greece.

**III** Colonization and Culture Contact.

**A.** Colonies are usually modeled on the society from which they originate. Through contact with other cultures, however, colonies can exert a profound influence on their homeland.

The close connection between trade and colonization confirmed this. Through trade, the Greeks came in contact with other cultures.

1.  This is illustrated by the introduction of writing. The Greek alphabet is adapted from a Semitic script, and the earliest examples of written Greek came from the Greek colonies in southern Italy.
2.  It is likely that the Greeks acquired their alphabet from contact with Phoenician traders whom they met in the eastern Mediterranean (Al Mina) and in the west (Pithecoussae and the Bay of Naples).

B.  Colonies exposed the Greek world to new ideas and religious systems, as well as new styles of art. The influence of Near Eastern, particularly Syrian culture, on the Greeks is so profound that this period is often referred to as the Orientalizing Period.

1.  This influence can be seen in the poetry of Hesiod (c. 700), who incorporates Near Eastern myths and religious ideas into his treatment of the Greek gods.
2.  This is also evident in Greek vase-painting and the plastic arts, both of which borrow heavily from Syrian models.

C.  For the past 50 years, the most fruitful area of classical Greek studies has been the examination of Greek linkages to the civilizations of the ancient Near East.

## Suggested Reading

Graham, A.J. (1964) *Colony and Mother City in Ancient Greece.* New York: Barnes & Noble.

Malkin (1987) *Religion and Colonization in Ancient Greece.* Leiden: Brill.

Dougherty, C. (1993) *The Poetics of Colonization. From City to Text in Archaic Greece.* Oxford: Oxford University Press.

## Questions to Consider

1.  In what ways did contact with non-Greek cultures influence the subsequent development of the Greeks?
2.  What role do indigenous peoples play in the world of the Greek colonies?

# Lecture Six—Transcript
## From Sicily to Syria—
## The Growth of Trade and Colonization

Welcome back to this, the sixth of our lectures on Ancient Greek Civilization. In the last lecture, in dealing with the period that came after the Bronze Age and looking at that dreadful period of decline that we usually call the Dark Ages, I tried to make the case that by about the eighth century B.C., the Greeks were reforming their culture and showing a new direction in the development of their culture. I pointed out that there are going to be many different manifestations of this, some of which we're going to look at in future lectures, such as the growth of the power of Delphi and Olympia—the origins of the Olympic Games, for example.

The two areas that we have looked at so far are the writing down of epic and the development of city-states (*poleis*). In the first of these, we saw that although oral poetry had existed for hundreds of years, there was a climactic moment toward the end of the eighth century B.C. when, for the first time, the Greeks began to write these poems down. I talked about the importance of these monumental versions of the *Iliad* and the *Odyssey*, these poems going back to the Trojan War, and their subsequent impact on the Greeks as they used these as the basis for a moral code and the education of young men.

We also looked at the rise of the *polis* and at the growth of these larger communities, which are really very unlike the palaces of the Bronze Age. They are also very unlike the *oikoi* or households of the Dark Ages. This is something new. It is made of a combination of households, into village, into hamlet, into town, and so forth.

There is one other great aspect of change in the Greek world in the eighth century B.C. that I'd like to concentrate on during this lecture, and that is trade and colonization. In other words, we're going to look both at the causes for these—why did the Greeks trade and where were they founding their colonies and why—but then also I want to ask some questions about the impact of these. What is it in the eighth century B.C. and onwards that we see the Greeks getting from their colonializing experience and from their contacts with other cultures through trade and colonization?

A word of caution at the outset: when I use a term like "colonization," our tendency normally is to think in terms of the kind of colonial experience of the 19th century. Probably you all, like me, grew up with maps of the world that showed various regions of the globe that were color-coded according to the western European country that in the 19th century had staked a claim to that particular territory. The sun never set on the British Empire. There was always a red bit somewhere on that globe where you could see still a British colony.

The colonial experience of the Greeks was very different. This was not something initiated by large nation states or by the Greeks in general. It was not designed to annex large areas of territory such as portions of Africa or of Asia at all. It was certainly not designed to take a native population and to turn them into the labor force for an expanding capitalistic economy. The colonial experience of the ancient world is of a completely different style and nature.

The Greeks, in fact, have ever been exporting their people. If you go to either Toronto, Chicago or Melbourne today, in any of those three cities you'll be faced with the claim that that's the largest Greek-speaking city outside of Greece. Like the Irish, the Greeks export their people, leaving Greece constantly. This happened in antiquity as well, as Greeks left their homeland.

Particularly around 700 B.C. and on, there was a fresh wave of colonization which was quite different from the waves that came before or after. It led to the founding of a number of Greek colonies all over the Aegean, and more particularly the Black Sea and the western Mediterranean as well. We're going to end up with colonies of the Greeks as far apart as Massilia in southern France (that's Marseilles), Baria in Spain, and Cyrene, still of the same name in north Africa. My favorite of all the colonial foundations of the Greeks, a colony whose very name I think sums up the major reason the Greeks colonized it, is called Olbia. It's in the Ukraine and its name simply means "wealthy."

Why were the Greeks sending out colonists to so many different parts of the Mediterranean? Most of the colonies that we end up with are very close to the sea. The Greeks rarely penetrate inland at all. Invariably, their colonies are located close to a good, rich supply of soil and to large stretches of fertile land that are well-watered. I think this, though it may seem very obvious, helps to explain what Greek colonization is primarily about: it is the desire to get rich land.

If you've been to Greece and traveled around Greece, you'll understand why it should be that this is a constant in Greek history. In Greece, you'll be told that as God created the world, he walked around with a sack on his back and he distributed rich fertile fields, well-wooded mountain sides, and lovely rivers all over the world to the different countries of the Earth. When he got to Greece, he looked in his bag and all he had left was rocks. As a result, all the Greeks can farm is rocks.

That's a slight exaggeration. There are, in fact, some quite fertile stretches of land in Greece. However, it is true to say that the good land in Greece tends to be contained in small pockets. It is probably the case that throughout their history, many Greeks in these areas reached a population level that got to the absolute amount that the land could sustain and that then there was pressure on people to leave.

There are other factors that play into this as well. For example, if you have a system where eldest sons inherit the land because there is only so much land that can be divided, then there are going to be younger sons left over who have to be taken care of. In the way that younger sons of the British Empire might join the church or the Indian army and serve the Raj, here in the Greek world, younger sons will often take part in colonial expeditions and join a new colony. Why have no land back in Greece, where your older brother has five acres, when you can take off to southern Italy and there have 30 acres of prime farming land?

There are certain factors here that I think are quite constant and are carried over from generation to generation.

We have one document that gives us something, I think, of an insight into the way the Greeks felt about this issue of the use of land during their colonial experience. It's in the *Odyssey*, in an episode that you may find surprising. You know, of course, that in the *Odyssey*, at one point when Odysseus is relating his adventures, he talks about visiting the land of the Cyclops. The episode is a well-remembered one because the Cyclops is this extraordinary creature with one eye in the center of its forehead. Odysseus, you'll recall, outsmarts him. He gouges out the eye while [the Cyclops is] drunk. Odysseus then hides underneath the ram and he manages to escape under the belly of the ram. All the time he's been telling the Cyclops that his name is "nobody," so that when everyone says to the Cyclops, "Who is hurting you?" he replies, "Nobody's hurting me." As a result, Odysseus is able to escape.

There's a whole other element in that story that is often passed over and that I call to your attention. Odysseus gives us a long description of what it was like to sail first into the Cyclops' land. What he says is that "We came to the land of the Cyclops, who were lawless. They were lawless and they had no community, no *agora*, and no meeting. Instead, each one of them separately lived up on the heights in his own cave and each one separately gave his own law to his wife and children."

This is an image of a barbaric people who have no sense of community. Odysseus says that when he came to their land, he was appalled by the fact that just offshore from the land of the Cyclops, there was the most glorious island that had well-watered meadows and rich subsoil beneath. It was crying out to be colonized and to be used. Says Odysseus, "Only wild goats had it. There were no hunters there, no hunters' tracks across the hills at all." It was land that was in his eyes virgin territory and it was unused. It is clear in the poem that Odysseus, and I think Homer too, is appalled at the prospect of there being this good rich land that is going to waste.

He says, "The Cyclops have no clever craftsman who will fashion for them ships with red prows, the sorts of ships by which they can cross the water as we would, crossing the seas to go from the cities of men to the cities of men." This is a description that clearly comes out of a time and context when the audience for the Homeric poems in the eighth century B.C. is thinking about how wonderful it would be to go to a land where there was rich soil just ripe for the plucking. It is like the opening up of the west in this country's history.

Colonization left a big imprint on the Greeks, both as they contemplated the relative poverty of their own land and as they thought of how much was waiting for them if only they could sail out into the great unknown of the Mediterranean.

There was another factor that played an important role here, and it's one that I think we have to bring out. You remember that in an earlier lecture, I talked about the rise of the *polis*. I emphasized that in the eighth century B.C., around the same time that colonization is going on, smaller communities are growing into larger communities.

Individual households are giving way to larger communities of towns and even proto-cities—city-states (the *poleis*).

I want you to think for a moment about some of the problems that that may create for the people of the Greek world. If you live in an *oikos*, authority is clear. The head of the household is the law, whether it be the clan leader or, if he's gone, his son. What happens when two, three, four, or a dozen households all have amalgamated, living close together and forming a small town? What happens is that authority and justice are no longer a matter of the simple dictates handed down by the head of a household. These are issues that must be negotiated between heads of households. The first problem that faces a community larger than a tribe is that it should find institutions for justice.

I told you a story a moment ago about God giving the Greeks rocks. There is another expression, or story, I was told in Greece and that is that when you have six Greeks in a room, you have 12 opinions. In these early communities, there was a great deal of friction. As these families and these households are rubbing up against each other, these communities are trying to work out where justice lies. Who has the sanction of authority? Who can determine and give a judgment in a legal case? If my brother and I dispute over something, we can go to our father and he'll settle it. But when my neighbor and I dispute over it, what is the mechanism by which we can determine whether that land is mine or whether that land is his?

We find in the eighth century B.C. and through into the seventh and later into the sixth B.C. as well, that the birth of the city-state came with a great deal of pain. This is a pain that the Greeks called *stasis*. It means "conflict" and it is virtually a continual and ever present condition in the Greek city-state in its early history. People quite simply are endlessly fighting with each other. They are like the Montagues and the Capulets of *Romeo and Juliet*: great clans with their various retainers and their loyalties beating each other up every time they happen meet in a public space.

How does this link up with colonization? I would argue, and many have argued before me, that in the conditions of *stasis* (conflict) which prevailed in the early world of the city-state, colonization is a safety valve. It is a way of siphoning off some of that troublesome population. It is a way, quite simply, of getting some of your young men off the streets and out into a whole new world—a new colony—that's set up for them elsewhere.

For a variety of reasons, then, involving both the ownership of land and the emergence of these new city-states, the Greeks find it agreeable to be sailing out from Greece and looking for new land for their colonies.

A single city would provide the founder of the colony, known as the *oikist,* the father figure, if you will, for the whole colony. But of course colonies could be made up of a mixture of Greeks from different parts of the Greek world. A mother city might announce that it was going to send out a colony and people would pour in from different parts of the Greek world to the mother city and take part in this new foundation. We end up with what originates as polyglot communities from all over the Greek world that then have a foundation myth and a charter from the Delphic Oracle, which gives them a kind of common identity. Instead of being people from Thessaly, people from the Peloponnese, people from Argos and people from Arcadia, they end up in Italy as Syracusians, Tarantines or whatever other identity they choose to have.

As the Greeks founded their colonies, particularly in the western Mediterranean—I'm speaking primarily here of Sicily and southern Italy—they came into contact with another important and powerful civilization which was similarly colonizing at the same time. These were the Phoenicians, who came from Tyre and Sidon on what would today be the coast of Lebanon. They founded around 800 B.C. their own great western colony. They called it *Kart-Hadasht*, which in Semitic means "new city." We call it Carthage.

I call attention to the presence of the Phoenicians here because what we're going to find is that, in their colonial experience, the Greeks are going to brush up against the Phoenicians time and again. I think sometimes, because we're so used to thinking of Phoenicians in terms of the Punic Wars—the conflict between the Phoenicians, the Carthaginians and Rome later on—we tend to assume that this must have been a hostile experience—that Greeks and Phoenicians must have been almost ready to fight each other wherever they met.

In fact, I think the evidence suggests that the colonial experience for the two of them was not quite that hostile at all. There were places where colonies grew up that had begun as trading ports where both

Phoenicians and Greeks were side-by-side. We have such places, for example, at Pithecoussae in the Bay of Naples, where we have both Greeks and Phoenicians, and at Al Mina in northern Syria, where we again have Phoenicians and Greeks.

These places, Greek and non-Greek, settled side-by-side and traded together. From there and from this experience of trade, the Greeks established a series of trade routes, particularly leading up the Adriatic and across to the toe of Italy, to Sicily and around through the straits of Messina, where the Greeks sailed looking for resources (precious metals and so forth). These are the trade routes that they originate with, then colonization follows. It's not an either/or proposition. The two go hand-in-hand quite well.

Why? Quite simply because as a trader is sailing around the Mediterranean from port to port, he cannot help but see an island, inlet, or alluvial plain where there is no native population or where they look as if they could be easily beaten. On a trip back to Greece, all it takes is one report saying, "Gee, in Sicily, you know, I saw this place that really is ripe." There you have the process of trade leading on into colonization. It's a very natural feature of Greek history in the eighth century B.C.

This confluence of trade and colonization I think can be seen most clearly in Italy and in Sicily, particularly at the Bay of Naples. Here you have trade routes coming down from northern Europe into the Mediterranean and trade routes coming across from the western Mediterranean—these are intersecting. This is the same place where Greek traders will soon be followed by Greek colonists as well.

Let's assume, then, that we can say satisfactorily that trade and colonization go hand-in-hand and they're bringing the Greeks out of Greece into the wider Mediterranean world. What really interests me is not why they go out, but rather what happens to them as a result of this experience? Here, I think, we're going to be able to say something significant about the Greeks of the eighth century B.C. and the seventh century B.C.

Trade and colonization brought the Greeks into close contact with a number of other, older cultures, particularly that of the Phoenicians. It is hard to underestimate the impact of this cultural contact in the eighth and seventh centuries B.C. I want to illustrate now some of the ways in which I think in concrete terms the Greeks were affected by this contact with a non-Greek world.

The first and most obvious is one that we've alluded to a couple of times already in lectures, and that is writing. You remember that the Greeks of the Bronze Age wrote in Linear B. You remember that at the end of the Bronze Age, the practice of writing disappeared. There were no palaces. There were no records to be kept. Writing was not needed. Around 725 B.C., writing makes its way back into the Greek world once again, but the Greeks are no longer using the script of Linear B. They are using instead what we call the alphabet—the Greek letters of the Greek alphabet that they used for the rest of their history.

Where did it come from? The answer is that the Greek alphabet is borrowed from a northwest Semitic language—a language spoken either by the Phoenicians or by their near neighbors. I'm not saying that the Greeks started to speak Phoenician. Let's be clear about this: they're still speaking Greek. What they are doing is deciding toward the end of the eighth century B.C. that it would be useful to have a system of writing their language down. The system that they use for that is a system that originates as a Semitic language.

The Greeks do something subtle here, though. They make quite a change, because they take words in Semitic, like *aleph* and *beth*—things that mean "ox" and "house"—and they drop the meaning of the word and instead they simply take the sound. *Aleph* becomes the letter alpha, which is simply used to write down "ah"—not a word, not a meaning, not an object, but simply a sound. *Beth* loses its meaning as a word and it becomes merely to the Greeks the letter beta, which can be used to stand for the sound "buh."

With that quite extraordinary step of taking an existing system, dropping out the meanings associated with these symbols and making them purely phonetic, what the Greeks have done is borrowed someone else's writing system and very soon adapted it, using only between 24 and 27 letters, to write down everything in Greek. It is a system which does not require hundreds and thousands of ideograms or pictograms and, with only 24 to 27 letters approximately getting all the sounds of Greek, you can write down all of Greek with those letters. That's quite a breathtaking step if you think about it. It's really quite extraordinary.

Let's take this idea of the origins of writing a little further. I'm using it here to illustrate the notion that the Greeks really did acquire a great deal from their cultural contact with the broader world in which they were trading and colonizing. In relation to the acquisition of writing, some scholars have recently argued that what we should pay attention to is what the Greeks choose to write down first of all. What did the Greeks first write down once they had this alphabet? The answer is quite simply Homer. That's what Greek is being used for the first time we have Greek.

It's fairly clear, once again, that the Homeric poems have come to achieve an astonishing status if the very first thing that your entirely new writing system is used for is to record Homer—to write it down. I want to point out another aspect of the writing and that is not the question of what is written down, but rather where is the first Greek writing?

The answer is that our first pieces of coherent and lengthy Greek of any sort are not found in Greece. They're found in Pithecoussae, the Bay of Naples and Al Mina. Look at that: trading emporiums—places where the Greeks were trading and living right next door to the Phoenicians.

Can we go any further? Probably not with confidence. You might like to speculate on something like, "What happens when a Greek population and a Phoenician population live cheek-by-jowl for a generation or two?" The answer is you produce bilingual children, because men and women will have children and these children will grow up with both languages. Imagine a child growing up with both Phoenician and Greek, being literate in Phoenician and using that system to write down Greek. I happen to like the theory of the bilingual child as the source of the Greek alphabet. We can't prove it of course, but I throw it out for your delectation.

If we go beyond writing—if we use writing merely as the most concrete example of what the Greeks are getting from their exposure to the wider world of the ancient Near East—and ask, "What comes with that, not just in concrete terms, but intellectually, spiritually, and culturally on the more abstract level?" I think we get a very interesting answer.

The other poet of the eighth century B.C. whose work is of immense importance to the Greeks, aside from Homer, is Hesiod. Hesiod writes two long poems, *The Theogony* and *The Works and Days*. In *The Theogony*, he talks about the origins of the Greek gods. Later, people would say Hesiod in a sense codified the Greek gods. He taught the Greeks who their gods were.

When you read through the poems of Hesiod, you find something very interesting. We have, for example, the story of different generations of the gods. Originally, there is the god Uranus, who is attacked by his son Kronos. Remember, his genitals are cut off. Later, we also have then Kronos being deceived by his son, Zeus, who feeds him a rock to eat instead of himself being cannibalized by his own father. It's three generations of the gods, each generation overwhelming the generation that came before: one by physical attack and one by deception. That pattern is borrowed directly from an ancient Near Eastern poem, the *Epic of Kumarbi*.

We know it in a purely Greek form. The names in it are entirely Greek, the poet is Greek, and the language is Greek, but the structure, the plot line and the very story of the gods involved is not Greek. It is ancient Near Eastern.

In the same poem, *The Theogony*, the different generations of the gods lead us forward eventually to Zeus, who at the end of the poem, in order to confirm his power, must battle the giants. He must destroy, humiliate or bury these earlier more elemental forces who threaten that which is called the "will of Zeus" or the "justice of Zeus." The poem, in other words, is taking us from a more wild, elemental stage of monsters and earth through to a kind of anthropomorphic, very human looking, male, kingly god. The same pattern was recited in a poem every New Year in Babylon to the god Marduk in the Babylonian creation epic known as the *Enuma Elish*.

What we're finding in Hesiod, quite frankly then, is the way in which Greek culture in the eighth century B.C. was deeply permeated with the thinking, religion, and sensibility of the ancient Near East. You can say the same thing when you look at the actual material arts of the eighth century B.C. and look at the bowls, for example, that are being exported from Syria to Greece. At every level, at the most concrete in terms of objects and at the most abstract in terms of ideas, the Greek world of the eighth century B.C. is deeply immersed in the ancient Near East. It is for that reason that people so often speak of this as being an "Orientalizing Period"—Orient simply in the terms of further east than Greece. It is a veritable revolution in the way the Greeks see the world.

I want to finish by briefly bringing you up to date on why I have emphasized this deep connection with the ancient Near East so emphatically. It's because in recent years classicists and ancient historians have been charged with a continuing and ongoing racism that is supposed to have originated in the 19th century when white historians tried to systematically write out the ancient Near Eastern and African roots of classical culture. In the work of some scholars, it is argued that we are still doing the same thing today—denying that the Greeks had Afro-Asian roots.

I want to suggest to you that in fact, for at least the last 30 if not 50 years, the most fruitful line of inquiry in ancient history—in Greek history for this period—has been precisely to explore the deep debt of the Greeks to particularly the world of the ancient Near East.

In both the Bronze Age and now in this period—in the Iron Age and particularly now in the early Archaic period—what we're seeing is the same fundamental truth of Greece's location. It is not, for most of its history, a unique area—the cradle of western civilization unique unto itself. But throughout its history, both in the Bronze Age and coming up into the Classical period, it will be intimately connected to, a part of, and influenced by its ongoing connections to the world of the eastern Mediterranean.

# Lecture Seven
# Delphi and Olympia

**Scope:**

The two most important institutions to emerge in Greece before the Classical period were the oracle of Apollo at Delphi and the Olympic Games. Both were Panhellenic institutions, open to any person or community identified as Greek. Such institutions were crucial in fostering a Greek identity in the face of political fragmentation.

At the same time, both institutions reinforced the strong tendency towards separatism among the Greeks by favoring a highly competitive, "agonistic" environment. The *agon*, or contest, became a dominant feature of the Greek experience. It influenced the Greek conception of both personal relations and political life.

Together these institutions fundamentally shaped what it meant to be a Greek.

# Outline

**I.** Delphi and the Oracle of Apollo.

    **A.** The sanctuary of Apollo was far more than a single temple or altar.

        **1.** It was not comparable to a church. Rather, it was a sacred space that included both temple and altar, as well as temples of other gods, treasuries, dedications, and offerings.

        **2.** The Greeks regarded Delphi as the center of the universe.

        **3.** The god possessed and spoke through the priestess.

    **B.** After 800 B.C., the number and value of the offerings at Delphi increased dramatically, demonstrating that the sanctuary was quickly gaining prestige beyond its immediate area. Treasuries were established there to store the goods contributed by various Greek communities.

    **C.** Located in the center of Greece, Delphi attracted suppliants from all over the Greek world. As city-states grew and colonies were established, Delphi came to play the role of mediator in Greek affairs.

1. Official embassies requested oracles on behalf of their states. The oracle shaped the policies of state officials who consulted it.
2. Delphi grew in status and authority as it authorized the founding of colonies.
3. Delphi offered judgments in interstate disputes and settled quarrels over borders.

D. This mediation was made possible by Delphi's neutrality. The sanctuary was administered by the priestly clans of Delphi in conjunction with a religious confederation of the Greek states. Delphi served the entire Greek community, not just one particular state.

II. Olympia and the Panhellenic Games.

A. The Olympic Games were the first of a series of four Panhellenic contests, founded in 776 B.C. and open to all Greeks.

1. Like Delphi, Olympia was a religious sanctuary (to Zeus) and therefore neutral. It grew into a religious and athletic complex. The Games were protected by a Sacred Truce.
2. The modern Olympics, by contrast, have a nationalist focus, and they are heavily affected by international politics.

B. Although less tied to the foundation of colonies or the settling of disputes, Olympia became Delphi's equal in prestige for its athletic competitions.

C. The Olympic Games express the agonistic spirit of the Greeks at both the individual and communal level.

1. Athletes competed to display their *arete* or excellence, the same quality valued by Homer's warriors. Athletes sought the Homeric prize of *cleos aphthiton*—undying glory—for themselves, their families, and their communities.
2. The games were originally the venue for aristocratic competition between men (and boys) who explicitly modeled themselves on Homer's heroes.
3. As city-states emerged, athletes competed on behalf of themselves and their community.

**4.** As with Homeric heroes, the deeds of these victors are commemorated in verse, winning them "undying glory." The Boeotian poet Pindar wrote odes celebrating Olympic victors and the exploits of their relatives. The odes connected the contemporary winner to an antique "golden age."

**5.** The Homeric code was enacted and displayed at Olympia.

**III.** Unity, Competition and Strife.

**A.** The Panhellenic Contests allowed Archaic Greek society to define itself not as a nation, but as a culture made up of separate and distinct political units, united by their participation in these common contests.

**1.** The Greeks became Greek by competing with other Greeks. Inclusion in the Games confirmed one's Greekness.

**2.** According to Herodotus, those are Greek who share a common blood, language, religion, and customs. Only the first of these, however, is exclusive. The idea gradually emerged that to be Greek, one must live and act as a Greek—especially by engaging in competition with others.

**3.** Hesiod distinguished between "good" *eris* or strife, which encourages one to do well for himself in a way that does not hurt others, and "bad" *eris*, which encourages envy. Both are at the core of Greek life.

**4.** The Greeks needed to find institutions and cultural forms that would help them to move beyond their addiction to competitive strife. They failed to develop these institutions at the international level.

**B.** Delphi represents the reverse of the coin. The oracle at Delphi was the only permanent institution of the Greeks capable of mediating the permanent state of conflict that existed among the Greeks.

**Suggested Reading**

Morgan, C. (1990) *Athletes and Oracles. The Transformation of Olympia and Delphi in the Eighth Century B.C.* Cambridge: Cambridge University Press.

Rolley, C., Jacquemin, A. and Laroche, D., eds (1990) *Delphes. Oracles, Cultes et Jeux*. Les Dossiers d'Archaeologie 151 Dijon.

## Questions to Consider

1. What is the relationship between the panhellenism implicit in Homer's poems and the agonistic spirit institutionalized at Olympia?

2. How successful was Delphi in providing mediation to the interstate conflicts of the Archaic period?

# Lecture Seven—Transcript
## Delphi and Olympia

Welcome back to our series of lectures on Ancient Greek Civilization. In our last two lectures, we concentrated on some of the most important changes that took place in the Greek world during the eighth century B.C. You will recall that we paid particular attention to the rise of the *polis*, as the household units (the *oikoi*) of the Dark Ages gave way to larger and larger agglomerations: hamlets, villages, and towns.

We saw also that as *poleis* began to evolve, there were other important changes taking place in the Greek world at the same time. For example, we saw that at the end of the eighth century B.C., sometime around 725 B.C., for the first time the poems of Homer were written down. This was significant both in terms of what it meant for epic poetry and for what it meant for the Greeks now that they were equipped with a writing system.

We saw also that that writing system had been borrowed from the Near East. They were using an adapted version of a northwest Semitic script. In discussing this, we talked about the incredible influence, during the Orientalizing Period, on the Greeks from the ancient Near East. It was an influence that was felt as the Greeks sent out colonies and traded around the eastern Mediterranean and indeed Sicily, Italy and the western Mediterranean as well.

This period of great change in the eighth century B.C. also saw astonishing developments at two of the most important religious sanctuaries in the ancient Greek world: Delphi and Olympia. It's the particular changes that take place there and the significance of these changes that I want to talk about in today's lecture.

Let's look first of all at Delphi. Delphi was far more than a simple temple to Apollo and far more than an altar where sacrifices were made in his honor. It would really be wrong to think of it in terms of modern analogies to a church or a synagogue. Rather, the sanctuary of Apollo was a sacred space—an entire area set aside for the god. It was a place that held an altar, where sacrifices where made in his honor, and a temple, but in addition to this, the entire sanctuary was littered, quite literally, with treasuries where dedications made in honor of the god were stored and where dedications could be put on display.

Delphi also is different in that it is the one place that the Greeks regard as the center of their universe. It is what they call the *omphalos*, the "navel of the world." To them, it is the very center, not just of Greece, but of the entire world.

The particular worship which took place at Delphi is quite extraordinary, because, unlike at other sanctuaries where sacrifices may be made and you would hope that the gods were paying attention to you, at Delphi you could be sure that the god was present. The god actually spoke through the priestess, whom he possessed. Our word "enthusiasm" in English comes from the Greek *enthousiasmos*, which means the possession of the god as he takes control of the body of the priestess and infuses her with his spirit, so that when she speaks, she is uttering his words. These words would then be written down by priests, rendered into good hexameter verse, and then given back to those who had approached the oracle.

Delphi is a charged space. It is the center of the world and it is the place where the divine is made manifest in human affairs.

Delphi really gives us a window onto the world of the eighth century B.C. because it is during that time that the number and the value of the offerings at Delphi increase dramatically. What one finds through the course of Delphi's history is that early on we will find fairly humble offerings on behalf of individuals gradually being replaced by more and more elaborate offerings, such as the great bronze tripods that we have. These finally give way to offerings and dedications not just by individuals, but by entire states. For example, if you go to Delphi into the museum now, you can still see the sphinx erected by the Naxians—not an individual, but an entire community imploring the god for his help or his oracle, and then thanking him by putting up a dedication in his honor.

Because various states were making these offerings to the god, it became necessary for them to build houses where they could store the various dedications. These were precious objects of gold and silver. We find that throughout Delphi's history, the sanctuary becomes more and more clustered with treasury houses that are put there in honor of the god to store the goods dedicated by states. The best known of these, of course, is the treasury of the Athenians, which was rebuilt early this century and can still be seen in the middle of the sacred way.

As Delphi grew in influence from the eighth into the seventh and sixth centuries B.C., suppliants came to it from all over the Greek world. As city-states began to grow, become larger and take part in the colonial movement of the eighth and seventh centuries B.C., Delphi came to play a role that was central to the affairs of all the Greek states.

This can really be summarized in three ways. First of all, officials came to Delphi on behalf of their entire state seeking a propitious oracle from the god. The best-known example of this, of course, is recorded in Herodotus. On the eve of the Persian invasions, the Athenians sent a state embassy to Apollo to find out what was going to happen to Athens. I'm sure that they were hoping that the god was going to say, "Don't worry, everything will be fine." Instead, the first words out of the priestess's mouth were, "Flee! You are all doomed."

In what I think is an extraordinarily insightful moment in Herodotus, we find the Athenian embassy going back to the god and asking for a second, better oracle, if he wouldn't mind. The god was obliging and said, in rather cryptic fashion, that "far-seeing as use to vouchsafe to this alone to his daughter, gray-eyed Athena that the wooden walls would stand fast." This, of course, then precipitated a further debate in Athens as to what the hell the wooden walls were. Some people said it was the hedge growing around the top of the Acropolis and believing that, they went to the Acropolis and hid out there. The Persians eventually slaughtered them.

Others, notably Themistocles, said, "No, the wooden walls are in fact the ships." The entire Athenian state, apart from those who stayed up in the Acropolis, actually departed, moving their women, children and goods across from Athens to Troizen. Then the men stayed on their boats, fought against the Persians and were of course eventually victorious in the battle of Salamis.

That's quite dramatic because what we find there is an entire state policy of the most dramatic kind—a decision to quit the city and let the city be sacked by the Persians—all predicated on the words of Apollo at Delphi.

This oracle had immense authority and immense influence on the affairs of the Greeks—not just of individuals who might approach the god and say, "Should I lend my brother-in-law $500?," but of entire states shaping their policy on what was said to them by the oracle of Apollo.

One of the reasons that the influence of Delphi grew so much in the eighth and seventh centuries B.C. is that it was particularly associated with one of the other great changes we've already talked about, and that is colonization. City-states that were planning on sending out a colony would approach Apollo. They would ask for his advice and ask for an oracle that would give them some idea as to whether or not it was right to send out a colony, perhaps where the colony should be founded and whom might be sent in the colonial expedition.

As colonization picked up in the eighth and seventh centuries B.C., so too did Delphi's authority. More than one historian has pointed out that colonization did more for Delphi than Delphi did for colonization. That is to say, it grew in status as a result of the number of colonies being spread around the Mediterranean.

Within mainland Greece and the Greek world, Delphi played a very important role as well, which also comes back to something we've talked about in earlier lectures. You know that we've been discussing the fact that the Greeks did not unite politically, but rather forged a common culture which they all shared. As city-states grew, there also grew problems between city-states. In fact, the city-states were continuously at war with each other.

Delphi provided one key element in this political equation of international relations. It played a mediating role between states. On occasion, it could broker peace. More particularly, it could settle disputes involving land, so that ambassadors from Delphi, for example, might actually view a contested border area and give it a decision as to which hill, which river, or which plain belongs to this city or to that city.

This role of international mediation and authorizing colonies all contributed to the immense status of Delphi. It played a very important role then in a world that was made up of fractured Greek city-states continuously at war with each other. This role of mediation was one that was made possible, in part, by the fact that Delphi was neutral. The sanctuary of Apollo was considered separate from the actual town of Delphi, which was in any case politically quite insignificant. The sanctuary was administered on a daily basis by various priestly clans, with whom you negotiated, for example, to buy animals that would then be sacrificed on your behalf. The entire sanctuary and its affairs, particularly its wealth and building accounts—its program of building new treasuries or more elaborate temples, for example—were controlled not by the people of Delphi, but rather by an international federation called the Amphictyony, a religious confederation of Greek states both from the north and the south.

It was, in a way, the only version of the United Nations that the Greeks ever came up with. It's interesting that it was essentially a religious body concerned with maintaining the independence of Delphi, so that unlike virtually every other sanctuary in the Greek world, Delphi was not a sanctuary controlled by the neighboring towns or the neighboring tribe. It was set apart and as such, it could then serve the entire Greek community.

The second great sanctuary, which underwent extraordinary changes in the eighth century B.C., was Olympia. In some respects, the story of what happens at Olympia is both an analogy to Delphi and also its inversion. Let me explain what I mean by this. The authority of Delphi, as we've seen, was primarily religious. The authority of Olympia was somewhat different. It was mostly associated with the great games that were held there every four years: the Olympic Games. These games were founded in 776 B.C. and they continued every four years for the next thousand years.

Nevertheless, Olympia was a religious sanctuary first and foremost. If you look at a ground plan of Olympia, you'll find there is a hippodrome where chariot races were held, and there are three different stadiums, one built on top of the other as the stadiums become larger and larger and as competition becomes more and more intense. But at the very heart of Olympia are not the stadiums, but rather the Temple of Zeus, or even more particularly or correctly, the altar on which sacrifices were made to Zeus. It is a religious sanctuary.

Like Delphi, it combined its religious function with an athletic function as well. Delphi also had its pan-Hellenic games, known as the Pythian Games. As at Delphi, the games at Olympia were protected by a Sacred Truce.

In certain respects, we have to think of the ancient Olympic Games as being utterly different from our modern version. Our modern Olympic Games are about individual athletes, but of course the games have a very heavy nationalistic fervor associated with them. At the victory ceremony, of course, it is the flag of the nation, not the family signet ring or the banner of a particular athlete that gets lifted up. It's the national anthem which is sung. As we know, the modern Olympics have often shown the effects of war and politics. Two Olympiads in this century were missed because of the Second World War. Two more have been seriously affected by boycotts.

The ancient Olympics tried to avoid this and in fact were conceived differently. First of all, there was a Sacred Truce that was declared throughout Greece. Ambassadors from Olympia made their way around Greece declaring this Sacred Truce, which was designed to end all interstate warfare during the period of the festival, so that athletes could travel to Olympia and could perform in a completely neutral atmosphere and setting. Secondly, the games that were held at Olympia not only were held in this religious setting, but originally were primarily about individual athletes, not their states, although that would change.

The Olympic Games, in fact, arise from a feature of Greek culture which will become more and more important from the eighth century B.C. onwards. That is the "agonistic spirit" of the Greeks. This term comes from the Greek expression the *agon*, which means the "contest." The notion that there is a contest at the core of life is really a central Greek idea.

Athletes at the Olympic Games, particularly in its early days, were competing to display their personal excellence—their *arete*, which is a Homeric term that refers to their manly vigor and their qualities as warriors. This is the same quality that Homer's warriors try to display on the battlefield. Furthermore, what the athlete at Olympia is trying to win for himself, his family or community is what the Greeks would call *kleos aphthiton*, which means "undying glory." This also is a phrase which is taken directly out of Homer.

The Games, in about 776 B.C., originally, then, are a venue for competition not between states, but between aristocratic men, and boys as well (these are age competitions, so there are boys' versions of these games). They will compete in running, jumping, boxing, wrestling, and chariot racing as well. They are doing so explicitly modeling themselves on a Homeric pattern.

This becomes clear not only when we consider the competition at Olympia, but when we consider what also arises from it. If you win at Olympia, the chances are that you will go to a poet and you will commission that poet to write an ode—a victory song—on your behalf. These victory songs are not national anthems at all, but rather they're songs—and we have many of these, particularly from the Boeotian poet Pindar—which celebrate the individual and his success at the Olympics.

They do so by tying the individual and his Olympic victory to two other elements. One will be the victories of his forefathers. Such-and-such will be said to be the grandson of a man who was victorious, and the nephew of an uncle who was victorious, in boxing or wrestling or what-have-you. These are heroic genealogies, if you will. The second element that we'll find here in the poems of Pindar will be a reference to mythology, where a myth involving the early history of either that family or perhaps of some other family will be used again as a way of connecting this contemporary man to a long-gone golden age.

What I'm suggesting here is that we have an extremely interesting pattern of ideas and behavior. It is this: Homer, as we know, has encoded the morality of the Greeks and taught them how to behave. At Olympia, what we will find is that that code is enacted. It becomes the place in the real world of the eighth century where people can display their Homeric sense of what it is to be a Greek and to be a man.

The one encodes; the other enacts.

What becomes particularly interesting in the history of Olympia is that this originates quite clearly in the world of aristocratic competition—men behaving like Agamemnon and Odysseus. But as city-states grow more and more powerful, they will have an investment in these victories as well. What originates as competition between individuals will eventually come to be competition between individuals representing their states. In that respect, the ancient Olympics become very much like the modern Olympics: freighted with competition between states.

What we've got, I think, at Delphi and Olympia are some of the tensions that we're seeing expressed in the eighth century B.C. world. These pan-Hellenic contests are what allow the Archaic Greeks—the Greeks of the eighth century B.C. and on—to define themselves as a nation. They provide them with a cultural context which acknowledges separate units across the Greek world, but also provides them with participation in a competition that is only open to the Greeks.

This is an important point: at one point, later on, around the beginning of the fifth century B.C., a Macedonian king applied to take part in the Olympic Games. He was originally rebuffed. He was rebuffed on the grounds that he wasn't a Greek. He then returned and provided an elaborate genealogy that outlined his family's history and he attempted to prove that his far distant ancestors had come to Macedon from Greece, so that in that respect, he was Greek. As a result of that, he was allowed then to compete at the Olympic Games. It was vitally important that you prove yourself to be a Greek in order to be included in the Games; then by participating in the Games, you further demonstrated your Greekness.

The people who deliberated on this—the people who decided whether you or you or you were Greek—were know as the *Hellanodikai*. Their name means the "judges of the Greeks." Inclusion in the games actually affirms that you are a Greek. What this, I think, draws our attention to is that in the eighth century B.C., there was some concern with defining exactly who was and who wasn't a Greek, and deciding what it meant to be a Greek. This issue of ethnic identity remains an interesting one in the modern world as well, particularly in societies like the United States, which have such diverse populations. The Greeks were thinking about this same sort of issue.

In Herodotus, we get a sense of what the Greek definition of Greekness is. Herodotus says that those who are Greeks share a common blood, a common language, a common religion, and common customs. Common blood should mean that people are actually born Greek because their parents were Greek. This is sort of a biological definition of being Greek. Notice some of the other definitions there as well. Greek language: presumably anyone can learn Greek, so that seems to open the idea that there may be a cultural definition of Greekness. Religion and customs similarly: in other words, to be a Greek, it's not enough to say that your parents are Greek and that your blood is Greek. You have to perform, live and act like a Greek.

For the Greeks, that essentially means competition. This idea of competition is not only key to Greek culture, it is probably also the key to what is both best and worst about their culture. Let me try and explain this. A couple years ago, a colleague of mine who teaches Japanese history approached me and asked me to join him teaching a class that would compare the classical Greeks and medieval Japan—the classical period of Japanese culture.

I liked the idea of a comparative approach. He then sort of threw me for a loop by asking me, "If you had to summarize the Greeks in a single line—if there were one poetic line that was somehow to get to the very core of Greek culture, what would it be?" That's a tall order, but after some thought, the line that did occur to me was a line that comes from Hesiod, Homer's contemporary in the late eighth century B.C., around the time that these changes are going on that we've been talking about. In one of his poems, Hesiod says, "All abroad the Earth, there is not one, but rather two kinds of competition"—of strife (the Greek word for it is *eris*).

He further goes on to define this and to say, "The first of these is the spirit of strife or competition that leads you to emulate your neighbor and his success." For example, it's mid-winter and you think you'll just sit cozily by the fire, but you look out and you see your neighbor off to the barn to make some baskets. When springtime comes, he'll be ready to go out into the fields and do more work, whereas you will have to spend your springtime doing the work you should have done in winter. Hesiod says that if you decide to copy your neighbor and do the same sort of thing so that you'll be as successful as he is, then that is a good kind of strife or competition.

The bad kind of strife or competition, he says, is that which leads you to envy your neighbor. I was made to think of this some years ago when a friend told me that he'd introduced a new technique for planting his vines in Greece. Toward the end of the season, his clusters were producing much fuller grapes than any of his neighbors. He came to the field one morning to find that all of his vines had been cut down. Some jealous neighbor was sending him a very clear message—a very Hesiodic message: we are in competition and I don't like your success.

This notion that life is a kind of a zero-sum game—if I win, you lose, and if you win, I lose—is absolutely at the core of all Greek affairs. It is at the core of their conception of drama. It is at the core of their conception of inter-state rivalries and politics. It will come to the fore in the fifth century B.C. in the catastrophic war between the Athenians and Spartans. I believe it also deeply informs daily life and the way that people think about their neighbors, their democracy and their state. In other words, if some other group advocates a certain policy, we must oppose it simply because they are our opponents.

The Greeks, then, became completely addicted to this notion of strife—a kind of rugby principle of life: if you see a head, kick it. It became, I think, most important for there to be some mechanism, institution or cultural forum that would allow them to move beyond this.

Within states, that was partly affected by the growth of democracy, where at least free speech allowed people to share their ideas. The democracy, in fact, did allay some of the competitive strife, which had been affecting the world of Archaic Greece and the aristocratic rivalry of factions within city-states.

But at the international level, the Greeks never really reached the point of being able to find a mechanism to get beyond this model of endless competition. The nearest they would get to it would be Delphi on a permanent basis, and then beyond that, during times of absolute crisis, temporary leagues would be formed. For example, when the Persians invaded, temporarily the Greeks were able to bury their differences and to fight off the Persian foe.

I think it's very instructive to note that when the Persians invaded, the Greeks knew of the coming invasion for years. It was only in the final months, as the Persians were descending into Greece, that they were able to bury their differences and form a united front opposing the Persians. Even then, they withdrew from northern Greece. They withdrew from central Greece, unable to form a united policy. If Herodotus is to be trusted, the only way that the Greeks were ever able to bury their differences sufficiently to face the Persians in battle at Salamis was when they were tricked into it. Themistocles sent a message to the Persians so that they would block both ends of the channel at Salamis and make it impossible for the Greeks to escape. It forced them to fight.

I think this is really going to be a central feature of Greek life. It's a thing that we're going to be emphasizing more in the coming lectures, but I want you to pay close attention to the conditions under which it is formulated here in the eighth century B.C. In previous lectures, we've asked the question, "To what extent does the Bronze Age continue to influence the affairs of the Greeks?" I suggested that continuity is a very difficult concept to quantify.

I go further now and say it is really the eighth century B.C. which is the critical period in the formulation of Greek culture. It is now that we find the emergence of the city-states. It is now that we see the Greeks being heavily influenced by the ancient Near East. It is now that we find the Greeks formulating once and for all the notion that to be Greek means to be in competition with the other Greeks. It is now that we find the Greeks also formulating the idea of pan-Hellenism—the idea that despite our differences, at some level—culturally, linguistically and even in our blood—we are all Greeks.

# Lecture Eight
# The Spartans

**Scope:**

From the eighth century onwards the Greek world underwent many far-reaching changes: colonization, panhellenism, and the growth of city-states shaped the future course of Greek civilization. These rapid and dramatic developments also led to profound tensions within many Greek communities. Conflicts between regional groups, clans, and even entire classes led to political violence often bordering on civil war.

Different communities found different solution to the threat of *stasis* (civic violence). In many parts of Greece tyrants, unelected leaders, seized power and quelled political conflict by imposing autocratic rule. Sparta followed a different course. By creating a rigidly hierarchical society dominated by a warrior elite, and by enslaving the neighboring region of Messenia, Sparta fashioned a society unique among the Greek states. In this lecture we will examine Spartan society and attempt to explain how it took shape.

## Outline

I.  Early Sparta.

    **A.** Down to the sixth century, Sparta had all the hallmarks of a vibrant, open society. The arts flourished and displayed sophistication in many genres.

        **1.** The poetry of Tyrtaeus and Alcman shows that the Spartans composed beautiful hymns and that Spartan choruses of young girls participated in choral contests.

        **2.** Terra-cotta masks from the temple of Artemis Orthia point to a lively tradition in the plastic arts.

        **3.** Funeral *stelae*—grave markers—from Sparta show men and women sitting side by side as partners and equals.

    **B.** Over a long period from the late eighth century down to the middle of the seventh, Sparta engaged in a protracted struggle with the neighboring region of Messenia.

        **1.** This struggle culminated in the subjugation of the entire Messenian population c. 650–600 B.C.

**2.** The Spartans became the masters of Messenia and reduced the native population to the rank of helots, or serfs. The Messenians thenceforth worked the land on behalf of their Spartan overlords.

**C.** The conquest of Messenia constitutes the defining episode of Spartan history.

    **1.** By incorporating Messenia within the area of their direct control, the Spartans made themselves masters of a vastly larger servile population.

    **2.** Subsequently, fear of the helots encouraged the Spartans to develop a close-knit social order directed mainly toward maintaining the status quo. All Spartan institutions were devoted to keeping the helots in subjection.

**II.** *Eunomia* and the Foundation of the Spartan State.

**A.** Traditionally associated with the legendary law-giver, Lycurgus, the Spartan constitution was regarded by conservative Greeks as an example *eunomia*, good order. This social order was enshrined in the Rhetra.

**B.** The Spartans had distinctive political institutions.

    **1.** Alone among the various Greek states, the Spartans retained a dual kingship.

    **2.** Administration was handled by 5 *ephors*.

    **3.** A Council of 30 Elders advised the kings and served as a court.

    **4.** All adult male citizens deliberated in a general assembly.

**III.** Spartiates, Perioici, and Helots.

**A.** Sparta had a more exclusive definition of citizenship than other Greeks had. Full citizenship was restricted to the élite, known as the Spartiates. The other inhabitants of the region, known as Laconia, were relegated to a variety of inferior statuses.

**B.** Other social groups had subordinate political status.

    **1.** Many neighboring communities, the *Perioici*, were allowed local autonomy but were subject to service in the Spartan army.

    **2.** Spartiates unable to meet their obligations to the community were relegated to the status of Inferiors, without citizen rights.

3. Supporting the entire Spartan system was a class of serfs, the helots. Each Spartiate was allocated helots who worked his land, leaving him free to train for war. The Spartiate's helot would accompany him into warfare.

IV. The Institutions of the Spartan State.

A. After the enslavement of Messenia, Sparta became a closed society. Social cohesion was maintained by raising boys away from their families and in age-cohorts.

1. The *agoge*, or educational system, trained boys to grow up as warriors.

2. The *crypteia*, or secret commission, dispatched boys to live off the land and learn physical endurance. During this period, the boys could kill with impunity any helot they came across.

3. Men continued to live with their peers, dining together in common messes called *syssitia*. Every member was required to contribute the produce of his own land to the mess; those who failed to keep up their contributions were removed from the *syssition*.

4. The ideology of equality within the Spartan élite is summed up by their collective name: *homoioi*, or equals. Their own equality was supported by the dramatic inequality prevailing throughout the rest of Spartan society.

B. The closing of Spartan society is also demonstrated by other changes.

1. On various occasions the Spartans formally expelled all foreigners (*xenelasia*), probably in order to prevent infection by new ideas.

2. Commerce was severely restricted by the use of cumbersome bars instead of coins. The Spartans feared that international trade would introduce new ideas into their state.

3. Laconian pottery was soon eclipsed by Attic pottery.

4. The vigorous tradition of choral poetry in Archaic Sparta failed to develop in the classical period, unlike at Athens.

## Suggested Readings

Cartledge, P. (1979) *Sparta and Lakonia: a Regional History 1300-362 B.C.* London: Routledge.

## Questions to Consider

1. To what extent is it correct to describe ancient Sparta as a totalitarian society?

2. How did Sparta avoid the civil strife and tyranny that afflicted most other Greek states in the sixth century?

# Lecture Eight—Transcript
## The Spartans

Welcome to this, the eighth lecture in our series on Ancient Greek Civilization. In the last couple of lectures, I've been trying to make the case that from the eighth century B.C. onward, the Greeks underwent a series of very profound changes which would help to dictate the course of subsequent Greek civilization.

Among these changes, we looked at the growth of trade and colonization, the writing down of epic for the first time, the growth of city-states, and also, at the same time, the growth of a panhellenic idea, which finds particularly vivid expression both at Delphi and Olympia.

These rapid and dramatic developments also lead to great tensions within the emerging Greek city-states—the new Greek communities. These conflicts were sometimes between regional groups. They were sometimes between different aristocratic clans. Some of our evidence suggests that at times, these conflicts may have involved entire classes—the wealthy versus the poor.

So endemic was this kind of civic violence, known usually as "*stasis*," that it afflicted virtually every Greek city-state. As a result, many states were forced to deal with this problem. Because there were so few mechanisms politically for resolving these problems of violence and conflict, what happened in many parts of Greece was that unelected leaders, whom we call "tyrants," simply seized power. Their control of the various Greek city-states was sometimes in fact beneficial, because on many occasions they brought during their rule 10, 20 or 30 years of relative peace and harmony to the Greek city-states. We'll be looking in a later lecture in particular at the career of Pisistratus, who resolved many of the conflicts of Archaic Athens simply by virtue of his 40-year rule.

Today, instead of looking at Athens, which we're going to concentrate on in many lectures in this class—it is really the core of Greek culture for the Classical period—I want to turn my focus aside and look at one of the other Greek city-states, Sparta. The reason for this is that eventually Sparta and Athens would come to represent two very different and conflicting trajectories in Greek culture. Sparta would follow a very different course not just from Athens, but from most of the other Greek states. The kind of society that it would create—though it grew out of a response to *stasis* and conflict—would look very different. It would be organized very differently and would have institutions which were quite unique in the Greek world. Sparta is going to look alien not only to us; it looked alien to the Greeks as well.

It created, finally, a rigidly hierarchical society, one that was dominated by a warrior elite. Therefore, in some respects, it looks more like Homeric society than any other Greek place. In particular, it is a remarkable social unit, because it is one of the few areas of Greece that physically and politically dominated to the point of enslavement its neighbors, in this case Messenia.

In this lecture, then, I want to concentrate on Sparta, look at how its history took the shape that it did, and what it was that was particular and peculiar in the institutions of the Spartans.

In the first place (and this is a point that is not usually made in textbooks, but I think it's an important one), down to about the sixth century B.C., Sparta really has all the hallmarks of a typical Greek society. It was, in fact, up until that time quite an open society measured in terms of having flourishing arts and being quite sophisticated in many genres. We have wonderful poetry from the Archaic period that comes from Sparta, particularly associated with Tyrtaeus, who tells poems of war, and Alcman as well, whose poems show for us Spartan choruses of young women performing in competition in honor of the gods. The choruses are often answered by a single voice. These poems and the competitions that go with them are really quite extraordinarily beautiful choral contests that attest to a very lively poetic tradition in Archaic Sparta.

Very close to the downtown of the city of Sparta was a temple dedicated to Artemis Orthia. The masks that we have that come from here are really quite unlike anything that we get in the rest of the Greek world, but show a tradition of working in terra cotta and the plastic arts that again is quite lively, sophisticated and individual in its style, in Sparta in the sixth century B.C.

There is another piece of evidence. I feel closely associated to this, because you see it so rarely in books, but I saw this for the first time in the Spartan Museum a few years ago. There are funeral *stelae*: these are grave markers, which are put up over the graves of dead men and women. The scenes that they depict are scenes that you would not call typically "Spartan", if you think of that in its English sense. The funeral steles show men and women sitting quietly hand-in-hand, obviously examples of very companionable marriages. That warlike quality and suppression of emotion that we associate with Sparta are really quite absent from these funeral markers. In many respects then, up until the sixth century B.C., Sparta is very much unlike what our traditional view of Sparta is. It's an open society and I think one that's artistically extremely vigorous.

The question then arises, quite simply, "What happened? Why did Sparta take such a different trajectory in the rest of its history?" The answer lies in a series of wars, the chronology of which is very complicated and I'm certainly not going to deal with those issues in this lecture. They were a series of wars that took place beginning in the late eighth century B.C. and going on through the seventh century B.C., when Sparta was embroiled in wars with the region that lies immediately to the west, the region of Messenia. These wars culminated in the subjugation of the entire Messenian population around the period 650–600 B.C.

The Greeks, as we know, fought wars endlessly with each other. In virtually every Greek war, the outcome was that whichever side was victorious held the field of battle and then retreated. Some form of negotiated settlement took place thereafter. In particularly brutal instances during the Peloponnesian War, states might end up being ransacked, with the men killed and the women sold into slavery.

In the case of the Spartan victory in the Messenian Wars, we have a very different result, virtually unparalleled in Greek history. That is, the Spartans appropriated Messenian territory. They simply took it over. What happened to the Messenians? The Messenians became a subject population. You can call them either slaves or serfs, depending on your choice of words. The Greek term that expresses their status is *helot*.

They are a subject population, then, the indigenous inhabitants of the area of Messenia west of Sparta. Many of them stayed on the very land where they had been born and grown up, but the land was now owned by Spartans. The original owners were reduced to a subject population who worked the land on behalf of their Spartan overlords.

This conquest of Messenia, in my opinion, constitutes the defining episode in Spartan history. While most other Greek states engaged in warfare and colonization, the Spartans in a sense internally colonized the Peloponnese, by making this territory Spartan. By incorporating Messenia within the area of their direct control, they made themselves the masters of a vastly larger subject population. It is that brutal reality which will define much of what develops in Spartan history afterwards.

Quite simply, the Spartans (who are an elite group within their own region) are afraid of this helot population. For the rest of their history, they must essentially live as a minority group of slave owners surrounded by a vastly larger slave population.

I think we get some idea of what the effect of this must have been like and what the tensions in Sparta must have been in an episode that is recounted by Herodotus. A Spartan by the name of Cinadon is about to lead a revolt in Sparta. The revolt is reported to the Spartan officials, who then call him in for an interview. In the course of this interview, the Spartan officials say to him, "How many people are involved in this? How many people are actually ready to kill the Spartans and to take part in this revolt?"

Cinadon goes to the window and he gestures to the *agora* (the marketplace) outside and he says, "How many of these are full Spartan citizens?" The Spartan officials look and count and they see there is a very small number out there. The rest are non-Spartans. Cinadon says, "Everyone out there who is not a Spartan would be quite ready to eat the Spartans alive and raw."

Whether the episode actually took place or not, I can't actually guarantee, of course. But what it reflects is the notion that Sparta after the conquest of Messenia became a closed society in which every focus of every Spartan institution was oriented toward the subjugation of that much larger Messenian population.

What we should do now is look in more detail at the organization of Spartan society in the Archaic and the Classical periods to try to determine what their institutions were and what was particular and peculiar about them.

The Spartan constitution was normally regarded as a most shining example of what the Greeks called *eunomia*, which simply means "good order." The Spartan state in the eyes of conservatives throughout the Greek world was a model of good order. It was a model of how society should in fact be organized.

It was associated with a single founding figure named Lycurgus. Like many other Greek states, the Spartans assumed that their order had not developed over many years, but had been given to them by one almost semi-divine figure. This *eunomia*—this good order—was enshrined in a document called the "Rhetra," which actually stipulated various orders as to the organization of Spartan society.

The way that society was arranged was unique and particular and it worked like this. The Spartans, unlike virtually every other part of Greece, had a dual kingship—two kings serving at any given time. The historical explanation for this is probably that at some early stage in Spartan history, there had been two quite separate groups, each with their own king, who had fused and some arrangement had been worked out whereby the two royal houses would continue in power. This feature always seemed to the Greeks to be something Archaic. The very fact that it looked so old and that it looked in some ways Homeric gave it kudos in the eyes of conservative Greeks everywhere.

The actual administration of most affairs on a day-to-day basis was not handled by the kings, one of whom was usually a war leader, leading the Spartan army in the field. Day-to-day administration was in the hands of a team of five known as the "five *ephors*." They were supported by a council made up of 30 elders. The council included in it the two kings, so we really have 28 elders and then the two kings. They serve for life and served as a kind of Supreme Court for the Spartan state.

Then, below that, there is an assembly made up of all the adult male citizens.

In many respects, this organization is not unlike that of other Greek states. There is the notion of popular participation of adult males in an assembly. There is the notion of a council which actually advises and helps organize the running of affairs. As always, this will be in the hands of elders. Then there is a core group of administrators who run the state from day-to-day. All of that seems in many respects to be quite orthodox, but what it is based on is a much more exclusive definition of citizenship than applied in any other Greek state. I want to talk for a moment about the different orders and the different statuses of citizenship that existed in Sparta.

Full citizenship—the ability to serve in the assembly and the ability to serve in the army as a full Spartan warrior—was actually restricted to a narrow elite. They are technically known as the Spartiates. They are the cream of Spartan society. The rest of the people living in Sparta and its immediate environs (the region which is known as Laconia in southeastern Greece) were relegated to various lower statuses below that of the Spartiates. Those who lived in the communities surrounding the town of Sparta were simply known as the "neighbors," or in Greek the *Perioici*. They were left a degree of local autonomy, but they were subject to service in the Spartan army and always were under the control of Spartan officers—of Spartiates, I should say.

Spartiates who were unable to meet their obligations to their community (I'll define what these obligations were in a moment) were then dropped to a lower status and lost their citizen rights. They were known as the "inferiors."

Below this elite group of the Spartiates, there then was an entire class of serfs made up of the people of Laconia who were not full Spartiates and the people, of course, as we've seen, of Messenia. The relationship between these helots and their Spartiate masters is quite simply that the Spartiate master has a land allocation—a property, ranch or station, call it what you will—and it is worked for him by this slave population.

Each Spartiate also has a helot who accompanies him into war as a kind of batman—a helper. On some occasions, the Spartan army will allow helots actual military service, which of course then will be rewarded by being released from servitude.

This very hierarchical society in which people had an absolutely fixed place hardly changed for 300 years. It was all predicated on the enslavement of Messenia and the closing of Spartan society. In order to maintain this rigid order, all of the institutions of Sparta, and particularly those associated with childhood and the lives of men, were predicated on this notion of creating an absolute superiority of the Spartiate class.

For example, children were raised not with private families or their parents, but rather were raised with other children of the same age. This is a system that's not unparalleled in other societies. The Masai have a kind of similar system which is also oriented towards age cohorts. Children proceed through their education living with the children of the same age, growing up in dormitories. Of course, in the Spartan system, the entire intention of this is that every minute of the child's existence should be predicated on honing his military skills—athletic and military training designed to make these boys hardier, stronger and more reliable as warriors.

In addition to this, while children were going through this educational system known as the *agoge*, they were also exposed to another institution of Spartan society, which is really quite extraordinary, known as the *crypteia*. It comes from a Greek word which means the "hidden thing." The *crypteia* is a kind of secret police that exists in Sparta. That secret police is really made up of boys as they are undergoing their training. It would be comparable to us commissioning young men who are in ROTC to go off as a secret police force. They are dispatched to live off the land and to learn endurance. They are sent away for weeks at a time with nothing but a single dagger and then told to survive on their own.

There is one other aspect of the *crypteia*, which is often remarked on in our ancient sources. That is that if, in the course of their wanderings and living off the land, these Spartan boys happen to come across a helot, they may kill him with impunity. This is, I believe, a kind of terror technique that makes sure that helots will always be on their land. They can be accounted for. If they are not penned up on the farm where they're meant to be at night and you come across them somewhere on the road, then they shouldn't be there, so they're killed. This is a hideous institution, but I think it's attested in the sources and I think it exists.

In order to further inculcate this idea that you as a Spartiate are really only one of a class, rather than an individual, you continue to live with your peers even when you become an adult. You dine with them every day in a common mess hall. This whole system is known as the system of *syssitia*, or "common mess halls."

The *syssitia* brings together many different features of Spartan life. On the one hand, it makes real the notion that you should live with your Spartan brothers, but it is also based upon an economic reality. To live in this common mess every day, you have to supply that mess with a certain amount of produce—of grain from your land, for example. That means that your land is worked for you by your serfs (your helots or slaves) and its produce is then handed over to the *syssition* (the mess hall that you're in).

If you cannot maintain your contribution to the mess hall, you are dropped. It doesn't mean you're just kicked out of the mess hall. It means you're dropped from being a Spartiate and you lose your full citizen rights. This system of common mess halls actually inculcates and reinforces the notion that you must have these slaves working the land and producing sufficiently for you to maintain your status and your rank in Spartan society. It is based on the coercion of this Messenian population.

Yet in the fashion of this Spartan elite, the ideology that this serves is summed up by the term by which the Spartiates address each other. They call each other the *homoioi* (the "equals," "partners" or "same as each other"). There is an ideology of complete equality in that elite warrior band whose status in fact is supported by the complete inequality that exists throughout the rest of Spartan and Messenian society.

This "closing," as I've called it, of Spartan society—this turning away from the artistic openness of the seventh and sixth centuries B.C.—to be replaced by this extraordinarily coercive system of the late Archaic and Classical period then leads to a number of other institutions as well, which are quite particular to Spartan society. For example, we know from Thucydides that at various times in Spartan history when foreigners were in Sparta doing business, the Spartan ephors would simply declare that every foreigner must quit the city. This is known as *xenelasia* (the "driving out of strangers or foreigners"). What it surely represents is a deep-seated fear on the part of the Spartans that foreigners would bring with them new and open ideas. Ideas are dangerous. They can change society.

The best-known example that we have of such an episode, and I think it illustrates the paranoia at the heart of Spartan society, occurs in the 460s B.C. In 460 B.C., a terrible earthquake occurred. As a result of the upheaval which took place in the aftermath of this, many of the helots went into revolt. They barricaded themselves onto the top of a place called Mt. Ithome, located in their home territory of Messenia.

The Spartans of course, had to deal with this helot revolt because if it was successful, it would have challenged all of Spartan society.

When the Athenians offered to send them help, claiming that they were well versed in siege warfare and would be able to help break down the walls on Mt. Ithome, the Spartans accepted that offer of help.

An Athenian general by the name of Cimon marched to Sparta and then on to Messenia with an Athenian army. Some time later, he was politely asked by the Spartans to leave. He was expelled. Here we have the Spartans facing a serious revolt from the helots, receiving help from Athens, but then actually choosing to expel the Athenians rather than to keep them there and help fight the helots.

Why? Thucydides is very clear about this. He says that the Spartans were afraid that the ideas that the Athenians brought with them—the ideas of democracy, equality and so forth—would lead to a revolution in Sparta. They worried that these ideas would infect all of the population of Sparta and Messenia and that the Spartiates would find themselves in a much worse situation than having a single revolt on Mt. Ithome.

Another way in which we can see this closing of Spartan society, if you will, is the way in which Sparta treats the question of the economy. One of the great changes that's gone on in the Greek world during the Archaic period is that the Greeks have started to mint coins. Minted coins, of course, make it easy for international commerce to take place. We've seen throughout Greek history that as international commerce takes place, so too ideas are passed between regions.

Very quickly the Greeks realized that if you had coins, which made it possible to barter very easily and to trade, it also would bring with it intellectual ferment. This is what the Spartans were attempting to suppress and so they suppressed coinage. They did not want floods of foreigners coming in and doing business in Sparta. In Sparta, rather than having small gold and silver coins, the Spartans kept to a much older practice of using long cumbersome bars that couldn't be carried in the pocket at all and therefore made trade and commerce extremely difficult to carry out. It was yet another way in which we see Spartan society trying to avoid the trends that could be seen in the rest of the Greek world.

What was the effect of this on the Spartans? I think it was finally catastrophic. It could be measured in the arts, for a start. Whereas in the sixth century B.C., we have wonderful lyric and chorale poems coming from Sparta, and in the Classical period we have extraordinary poetry being generated in Athens by the great Athenian tragedians, we have nothing from Sparta. It has become culturally dead, in my opinion.

Furthermore, think about the pottery and the plastic arts that we've seen earlier in Spartan history. From the sixth century B.C. onwards, as Athenian pottery is becoming more vigorous, being exported around the Mediterranean, and demonstrating an extraordinarily wonderful aesthetic sensibility, what do we find at Sparta to match this? Nothing. It has become a dead end.

There is a way in which it is possible to move between the arts, politics and history of a particular region to draw together a fuller picture of what is happening. In the case of Sparta, I think we can summarize it in these terms. We have here a society which appeared to be a model of stability and good order to Greeks outside of Sparta (particularly conservative Greeks who liked the idea of having a large servile population at their beck and call), but all of that is the image of Sparta that is projected to the rest of the Greek world.

The reality is far different. The reality is that we have here a society which, in a sense, has missed the opportunities that the Archaic period presented to the Greeks—opportunities to move towards a more vigorous form of political, cultural and artistic life. That closing of the Spartan mind, if you will, and that closing of Spartan society, can in my opinion be taken back to one single event: the Messenian Wars of the eighth and seventh centuries B.C.—the domination of one Greek people by another.

I'm not going to be so naïve as to suggest that the Spartans were the only people who had slaves. All of Greek culture had slavery and slavery, as we know, is an extraordinarily vile human institution. Yet there is something particular in the way in which it was conducted in the world of the Spartans. Quite simply, there was virtually nothing to distinguish between Spartans and Messenians. They are the same people. They are quite literally neighbors to each other.

In a way, the most deep and fundamental immorality and indecency of one Greek people enslaving their neighboring people to me is the great disaster of Spartan society. In some respects, everything that follows from this—everything that is disappointing, futile and makes

Sparta unworthy of admiration—simply derives from that one single reality.

# Lecture Nine
# Revolution

**Scope:**

The sixth century B.C. was a period of rapid change throughout Greece. More manufacturing, increased wealth, and a greater volume of trade fueled the growth of towns such as Athens and Corinth. These changes also contributed to social upheaval and widespread instability. Factional strife (*stasis*) was rife in many towns. Regionalism and clan-based conflicts produced anarchy and in many places made it possible for tyrants to seize power.

In Athens the population attempted to forestall such a crisis by electing one man to overhaul the existing laws and to mediate between the various groups in conflict. Solon would be remembered as the father of the Athenian constitution. As we shall see in this lecture, he met with mixed success, but he deserves nevertheless to be regarded a great statesman.

# Outline

I. Conflict and Class.

    **A.** In the sixth century we begin to hear of entire groups calling themselves *aristoi*, the "best men."

        **1.** This occurs at a time when the constant theme of Greek poetry is *stasis*, civil conflict. For Marxist historians, this suggests that the Archaic period was a time of class struggle.

        **2.** But where we have details of this *stasis*, it usually turns out to involve competing groups of aristocrats and their friends.

    **B.** Although the Archaic period was not a time of class warfare, the growing wealth of a few and the impoverishment of many poor farmers fueled agitation for political and economic change. The tensions of the period operated both horizontally (between competing factions) and vertically (between classes).

II. Solon and the *Seisachtheia.*

    **A.** In Athens we have evidence of such a crisis in the poems of Solon. Elected *archon* in 594, he claimed to stand as a shield protecting both the people and the powerful.

    **1.** Solon refers to removing the marker-stones that enslaved the land. This statement probably refers to his abolition of a system by which land was mortgaged, causing many farmers to fall into debt.

    **2.** Solon claims to have freed many who had been enslaved by the rich.

    **3.** He also claims to have brought back Athenians who had been sold abroad in slavery.

**B.** His reform program was called the *Seisachtheia* or the "Shaking-Off of Burdens."

    **1.** Many poor farmers had been reduced to the status of tenant farmers, owing a share of their produce to the wealthy landowners to whom they were in debt.

    **2.** If land were inalienable, as many suppose, the poor secured their debts with their own person, and were subject to seizure if they defaulted.

    **3.** It was this system of serfdom and the real threat of slavery that Solon abolished.

    **4.** There is no evidence that Solon redistributed land, but he did cancel debt-bondage, reduced or cancelled existing debts, and probably confirmed the ownership of land by the poor.

**III.** Constitutional Reform.

**A.** Although he had been elected to deal with an economic crisis, Solon used his time in office to promulgate a series of far-reaching constitutional reforms designed to strengthen the rule of law.

**B.** Solon attempted to formalize the rights and privileges of each class according to its wealth. Wealth, not birth, would be the criterion for a citizen's access to public office. Four census ratings were created (or perhaps more clearly defined) based on the produce of the citizen's land.

    **1.** Pentakosiomedimnoi   > 500 measures (wet and dry)

    **2.** Hippeis (Knights)      > 300

    **3.** Zeugitai (Yeomen)     > 200

    **4.** Thetes (Labourers)     < 200

**C.** A second constitutional reform was the publication of Athens' laws. As with the census ratings, some of which may have existed before Solon, this codification introduced regularity and clarity. There now existed a comprehensive code of Athenian law.

**IV.** Taking advantage of his authority, Solon introduced a slew of reforms designed to contribute to Athens' prosperity.

   **A.** He supported the agricultural sector by banning the export of all agricultural produce from Attica except olive oil.

   **B.** He supported the manufacturing sector by offering citizenship to foreign craftsmen who moved to Athens.

   **C.** He adopted the Euboean system of weights and measures, making it easier for Athens to trade throughout the Aegean.

   **D.** He formalized the distinction between public and private law.

**V.** Revolution and the Rule of Law.

   **A.** If Solon's work was meant to be a revolutionary response to the crisis of Archaic Athens, then it was a moderate revolution. It can be viewed in terms of its short-term goals and long-term effects. As a solution to *stasis* and conflict, Solon's reforms were a failure, since in the immediate aftermath Athens underwent a further period of faction-fighting, anarchy, and eventually tyranny.

   **B.** In the long term, Solon's reforms set Athens on the road to democracy by strengthening the rule of law. Public life, public office, the legal system, and many areas of economic life as well had been given a more formal basis, making possible the emergence of a strong Athenian state, and finally, the Athenian democracy.

## Suggested Reading

Hignett, C. (1952) *A History of the Athenian Constitution.* Oxford: Oxford University Press.

## Questions to Consider

1. Is there a consistent theme running through all the reforms attributed to Solon?

2. How compelling is the evidence for class conflict in Archaic Athens?

# Lecture Nine—Transcript
## Revolution

Welcome back to our series of lectures on Ancient Greek Civilization. In our last lecture, in dealing with the Archaic period, we looked at the way in which during the Archaic period the Greek world was afflicted by a great many different tensions.

In particular, we paid attention to the response to this on the part of one state, Sparta. We saw that by a process of what I've called an "internal colonization" of Messenia, Sparta moved towards becoming a closed society marked by an extraordinarily rigid hierarchy and social order. The effect of this was to create in the minds of many of the Greeks a model example of good order (*eunomia*) and stability.

We saw that in fact the reality was somewhat different. It was a coercive society and, as we're going to see in a later lecture, it was rendered quite fragile by the particular path that it took. It eventually would succumb to military defeat and would be eclipsed socially and culturally in the fourth century B.C., but that's for another lecture.

What I want to do today is go back to the Archaic period, but turn our focus away from the slightly anomalous position of Sparta and instead look at what was going on in the rest of the Greek world. Then I'll concentrate on the way in which Athens, the state that we know most about, responded to the tensions and challenges of the Archaic period, particularly in the sixth century B.C.

Around Greece at this time in the sixth century B.C., we see an increase in manufacturing, an increase in the volume of goods being produced, and an increase in the volume of the trade of goods between states. This, of course, leads to an increase in wealth as well. This then fueled the growth of various towns such as Athens and Corinth, but it didn't do so without problems. These changes contributed to a great deal of social upheaval and to widespread instability. Not only did the Greek states fight wars against each other, but throughout this period, they were faced with strife within their communities as well. We've seen that the term for this is *stasis*. It refers to civil violence and factional strife and was rife throughout the Archaic period across Greece.

In some places, it was fueled by, or expressed by, regional conflicts. In other places, it was more clan-based. In many parts of Greece, this level of violence and conflict within the states led to a seizure of power by one man, who the Greeks would call a "tyrant." We'll be speaking a little bit more about the best-known example of tyranny, Pisistratus at Athens, in another lecture.

In Athens early in the sixth century B.C., the population attempted to forestall just such a seizure of power and to find some way out of the crisis that was affecting them by electing one man to overhaul the existing laws and to mediate between the various groups in conflict. His name is Solon. He is often regarded as the father of the Athenian constitution. During this lecture, I want to look more closely at the program of reform that he initiated. It's particularly interesting to deal with Solon because he was also a poet. We know a certain amount of his program of reform thanks to his own poetry, much of which was recorded and preserved for us in Aristotle's work, *The Constitution of the Athenians*, a fourth century B.C. treatise on Athenian history.

Let's talk a little bit about what's happening in Athens in the early sixth century B.C. Solon will be elected archon in 594 B.C. and that will be the date that we're concentrating on. Around this time in Athens, as in other parts of Greece, we begin to hear of groups of men who refer to themselves as the *aristoi* (the "best men"). Of course, such an exclusive, elite term such as *aristoi* only makes sense if these people are trying to define themselves against some other much larger, and to their mind inferior, group. This will often be referred to in our sources as the *demos* (the "people").

Our sources tend to suggest that this *stasis*, or civil conflict, was in a way informed by a basic opposition between a wealthy elite and a much larger citizen body. Of course, for Marxist historians, this has meant that the Archaic period can be viewed as a period of class struggle. I'm not going to be pushing a Marxist line in these lectures and I certainly don't want to defend Marxism as a current political belief, which has been proved to be quite bankrupt, but I do want to draw to your attention that as a line of interpretation of understanding ancient societies, it cannot be ignored. That is to say, you have to address the fundamental question: what impact do the basic economic relations of a society have on the history of that society?

Marx would say where a man or woman stands economically is really the prime relationship that that person will have with the rest of his community. For many Marxist historians, the Archaic period is a period in which wealthy Athenians and Greeks are virtually at war with the poor—with the *demos*.

It's an attractive approach in some respects, and yet, the more historians have looked at specific instances recorded either in poetry or better still in the work of the ancient historians like Herodotus and Thucydides, the more that it appears that the real conflict was not between rich and poor, but rather between various competing aristocratic groups: one faction led by this clan leader and his supporters opposing, and opposed by, another faction led by another clan leader and his supporters.

The Archaic period, in my opinion, was not a time of class warfare, although it was a period in which the wealth of a few was growing and the impoverishment of the poor was increasing as well. There are, if you like, class tensions in the Archaic period, which will fuel agitation for political and economic change. This will result in *stasis*, reform or tyranny, which ever option the Greeks take.

I think that we can best say of the Archaic period that there are different sorts of tensions operating at the same time. I would express them this way. There are both horizontal tensions between competing aristocratic groups or factions, if you will, and there are also underlying tensions that are vertical between the wealthy and the poor.

It's in the context of exactly this kind of situation of multiple tensions between different groups and classes that Athenian society finds itself caught in the early sixth century B.C. In 594 B.C., in response to this, the people elect as archon Solon. In his poems, he immediately talks about protecting both the powerful and the poor (or the people). He talks about himself as a kind of shield between different packs of wolves, helping the ship of state to take a steady course (yes, he does mix metaphors, just as I have done in that comment).

He clearly sees himself as some kind of moderate trying to navigate a successful path of reform between the wealthy and the poor. What does that mean in concrete terms? What did he actually do apart from write poems? We know that Solon says in his poetry that he removed the marker stones which enslaved the land. What does this mean? It seems to be Greek practice that when land was mortgaged—in other words, when the farmer who owned the land had fallen into debt—this mortgage was expressed by putting a marker stone on the land somewhere which would show this (a *horos* inscription as it's called in Greek—a boundary inscription).

When Solon says that he removes these, he's not referring specifically to the act of lifting these stones up and carting them away, but somehow ending a system of mortgage whereby farmers were trapped in a cycle of debt. He also says in his poems that he had freed the poor who had been enslaved to the rich. He says further that he brought back to Athens Athenians who had been enslaved and been sent out of the land. When he talks here about slavery—about the slavery of the poor to the rich and people being sent from Athens (sold into slavery)—I don't think he's speaking figuratively at all. I think he's speaking quite literally.

The reason for this is that it looks as if land were inalienable. That is to say, people couldn't sell it. If they couldn't sell it, it meant that when they took out loans, the collateral that they had to offer was not the land, which could then be seized by a bank or a lender. It was their person. If loans were collectable on the person, then we have to imagine a situation where people were in fact being sold into slavery as a result of some economic crisis. The exact details of this are very hard to patch together because as I've said, we're basically dealing with poetry in which Solon explains his actions, rather than a clear narrative account.

The later historians who wrote about Solon refer to his program of reform as the *Seisachtheia*, which means the "shaking off of burdens." That word *siesa* is the same as "seismic": the shaking or earthquake of burdens. It looks as if something like the following is what happened in Athens in the sixth century B.C.: many poor farmers had been reduced to the status of tenant farmers—sharecroppers, if you will, to use a modern term. They owed a share of their produce to the wealthy landowners to whom they were in debt.

They are referred to in our Greek sources as the *hektemoroi*, which means the one-sixth share men. There's some debate as to whether they kept five-sixths of their produce and had to pay one-sixth to the landowner, or, of course much worse, did they only keep one-sixth of their produce and have to pay over five-sixths of their produce. Particularly if the latter is the case, imagine a situation after a couple of years of bad crops and a couple years of defaulting on loans, if land is inalienable as we suppose and the poor had secured their debts on their own person. Then we would face a situation where many poor were becoming not only poorer, but were slipping into slavery. That appears to be the system that Solon was trying to address and trying to change. It was this system of serfdom, the real threat of slavery, which Solon abolished with the *Seisachtheia*—this cancellation.

There is no evidence to suggest that Solon actually redistributed the land, but he did cancel the institution of debt bondage and, in addition to making it impossible for people to be seized for their debts, he also either reduced or canceled entirely existing debts. Of course, as with everything else in ancient history, there is debate in the sources about what actually happened there. Some sources say that he canceled them, so that Athenian society began with a clean slate in 594 B.C. Other sources say that he reduced the level of debt and by doing so, he reconfirmed the ownership of the land by the poor.

Although Solon had been elected to office primarily to deal with an economic crisis, he also used his time in office to promulgate a series of far reaching constitutional reforms. I'm going to be arguing that in some respects, even though he was elected as an economic reformer, it is these constitutional reforms that subsequently were much more important in the history of Athens.

What Solon attempted to do in his constitutional reforms was to formalize and make quite clear and distinct the rights and the privileges of each class of Athenian society according to its wealth. This may seem to us not to be very democratic, but in the context of Archaic Athens, it is actually a step towards democracy in this respect: wealth, not birth, would now be the criterion for a citizen's access to public office. If you were wealthy enough, you could hold an office in the Athenian state. It did not depend upon the name of your father and your lineage.

In order to make this possible, what Solon did was to create a series of census ratings, according to which each adult male citizen would have the amount of his wealth recorded. Based on his wealth, which was measured in terms of the produce of his land, he would then have access to a particular set of offices.

Let me outline what these are. The highest rank is my favorite term in all of Greek history: the *Pentacosiomedimnoi*. You're fortunately not taking an exam after these lectures. I always set this to my undergraduates to see how many ways it can be misspelled. The term *Pentacosiomedimnoi* is a long Greek phrase that means the "500-measure men." What that means is that the total value of the produce of your land, both wet and dry (wine, oil, grain and so forth), must come to 500 standard measures. If you have more than that, you're in what is essentially the super-rich class of Athenian society. In our society, this would be the people who pay the highest luxury taxes.

The second rank of Athenian society, measured now by wealth, is made up of those people whose wealth is not quite at 500 measures, but is higher than 300 measures. It's between 300–500. They are known as the *Hippeis*, which means the "knights." There's an obvious reason why that label should be used for them. That's because in ancient Greek society, owning a horse was a measure of great wealth. Calling a whole class of people the horse-owners or the cavalry class is a little bit like calling a wealthy group in our society the "kind of people who can afford BMWs or Mercedes." It is labeling people according to a very clear and definite symbol of their wealth.

Below this comes the third group. They don't quite make it to 300 measures, but they have more than 200 measures of wealth. They're known as the *Zeugitae*. The *Zeugitae* are the men who own a pair of oxen. *Zeugitae* means the "yeomen," or the "yolk men," if you like. If you can afford a pair of oxen but not a horse, it means that, to use very anachronistically our terminology, you're middle class rather than upper class, if you like.

Then, if you're below 200 measures down to zero (if you're quite poor, like a subsistence farmer, for example) then you're of a class known to the Greeks as the *Thetes*. These are laborers. They may own a little bit of land of their own, but probably not even enough land to keep body and soul together. They have to sell their labor and work for other people.

Access to various offices was pinned to this wealth. If you were of the *Pentacosiomedimnoi*, then you could serve as one of the archons of Athens, as you could too if you were a member of the *Hippeis*. On the other hand, if you were of the *Zeugitae* class, you couldn't go to that high level of public service, but you could serve on the council.

If you're a member of the *Thetic* class, the bottom group, you couldn't actually serve in public office, but you could still take part in the public assembly.

One's participation in government and in public life here is being determined by one's wealth. As I say, it appears undemocratic to us, but in comparison to what had existed, it is actually a step forward because it creates regularity and the rule of law. This notion of establishing the rule of law—of making it clear what the regulations are by which we live and are ruled, not the capricious decisions of one man or one magistrate, but a consistent body of law that we can all refer to and understand—this we take for granted as a part of our democracy. Yet there must come a point in a society's development if it is moving towards democracy when it establishes this very fundamental principle: that our laws will be spelled out and that we can point to the law and say, "Look, it doesn't say that there," or "It does say that there."

This idea of the regularity of law in order to enforce the rule of law is something that the Athenians owe to Solon. They owe it to him in the quite literal sense that it is Solon who publishes the laws.

Before this, the Athenians must, of course, have had various laws, but when you came before a judge or were seeking justice, it was not always entirely clear whether you could point to something that was written down or whether it was simply a common understanding that people had. Now, with the changes of Solon, there exists a comprehensive code of law in which everything is spelled out and published so that citizens can actually see quite specifically how they are being governed and what their rights are before the courts.

This, I think, is really the core of Solon's genius and the importance of his legacy to the rest of Athenian history. Yet it's not limited to that. There are other legal and economic reforms that go with the changes we've already outlined. I sometimes wonder how Solon in that year managed to get any sleep, because we have a kind of program of reform that we would be happy to see take place over a decade. Yet it's here being punched through in a single year.

Taking advantage of this authority that he has—this archonship in 594 B.C.—he introduced a slew of new laws which were designed to help the Athenian economy and to encourage its prosperity. For example, he banned the export of all agricultural produce with the single exception of olive oil. "What on earth does that mean?" you might ask.

It's something of an exaggeration, but it was widely believed that Athens in antiquity was not fertile at all. It is true that for much of its history, the population of Athens was so great that the Athenians could not feed themselves with their own grain. They often imported grain from other parts of the world. It appears as if Solon was trying to address that perceived shortcoming by saying, "No grain can be exported. We must grow enough for ourselves." It was never entirely successful, but nevertheless that was his intention.

The only thing that could be grown for export was olive oil. Athenian olive oil was prized in antiquity as it is still today. There was a combination here of a desire to keep enough land so that the Athenians could feed themselves and have a single, well-defined crop that would be designed for international trade.

He did give citizenship to foreign craftsmen who came to Athens to live. By doing so, he was clearly also trying to bolster the manufacturing sector of the Athenian economy. We see him paying attention to the agricultural sector and to manufacturing as well. Normally, in most states, if a foreigner moved to a new place, they would be given status as a resident alien. In later Athenian history, that would certainly be the case as well. By actually granting them citizenship, he's encouraging them to come to Athens and to bring their skills with them to contribute to the growth of the Athenian economy.

It's fairly clear that he had these kinds of reforms in mind with a view to increasing prosperity, because we see another change, which only makes sense with that interpretation. That is that there were various systems of weights and measures around the Aegean world. The Athenians had one of their own, but under Solon, they ditched this system and actually transferred to the Euboean system of weights and measures, which was much more widely used. We know from more recent examples—one can think of Germany in the 18th and 19th centuries—that to have very different systems of weights and measures inhibits the economy. It means that there has to be a transfer every time goods are moved from one place to another and they're measured by a new system.

If you go with a system which is internationally used, you share in the prosperity of that trade as it circulates. That's why the greenback is so popular around the world. It's the same reason. This is a strong economy; its currency is good.

In one other final area that I want to mention, that of legal reform, he formalized the distinction between public and private law at Athens. Again, this is something that we take absolutely for granted. There are certain mechanisms whereby you may take your neighbor to court and these are very different from the mechanisms by which, for example, a president might be impeached. These kinds of distinctions don't simply happen over night. They happen because at some point, a legal reformer recognizes the need to codify the law.

I think what we can say when we pull all this together is that we do have a genuine revolution in 594 B.C. with Solon, yet we have to be very careful in the way that we understand this revolution. In terms of the economic crisis that was afflicting Athens, it was a moderate revolution. He did not redistribute land, so it was one that was designed to tackle the effects of an iniquitous system, but not to dislocate the economy as it attempted to reform. In some ways, he puts me in mind of what's happening in Russia right now as that country is trying to work out the dilemma of how radical its reforms should be. Of course, there is a good argument to be made for Solon (or for Russia right now) that the more vigorous the reform, the more dreadful its effects would be on the people who have to suffer right now. You can see why there would be an inclination towards moderation.

His reforms, I think, can be viewed in terms of their long-term goals and their short-term effects. In terms of their immediate effects, Solon was actually quite unsuccessful. We know this because we know of the record of Athenian politics in the years immediately after Solon left. At the end of his archonship in 594 B.C., Solon very wisely decided that having instituted a body of reform, he was going to get out of Athens for 10 years. He decided to let the Athenians work out the details and he would not be around to be endlessly pestered for further action.

He traveled for 10 years after his reforms. We know that during that 10 years in Athens, there was a period, for example, of two years in which the faction fighting continued to be so severe that the Athenians could literally not elect an archon (ruler). The term in

Greek for the inability to elect an archon is *anarchia*—anarchy, quite literally, in its most immediate sense. They had no head of state for two years.

On another occasion within that decade after Solon, an archon was elected who, at the end of his year, rather than laying down his office, decided to stay on for a second year and threatened to do so for a third year as well. Quite clearly, this Athenian, Damasias, was flirting with the idea of establishing himself as the tyrant of Athens. It was only by dint of good fortune that the Athenians managed to avoid that.

In political terms, in the short term, the Solonian revolution did not actually bring further peace and stability to Athens. In fact, the period after Solon was even more fraught than it had been before.

However, I don't think it's in the short term that we should judge him, but rather in the long term: what happened to Athens throughout the sixth and then the fifth and fourth centuries B.C. following from Solon's reforms. To me, the great legacy of Solon is his strengthening and firmly anchoring in the minds of the Athenians the importance of the rule of law.

We think primarily in terms of democracy and oligarchy of whether power is shared by all the people, whether it is only held by a small group, or whether it is held by one man as an autocrat. In some respects, when we approach the Athens of the sixth century B.C., we should not bring to bear these ideas about the dilemmas of politics. Rather, we should think of an earlier level. Before a society can work out how many people are to share in its governance, it must establish the idea of the supremacy of law and that regulations must be obeyed by all. That notion of the strengthening of the rule of law is the Solonian legacy.

Public life, participation in public office, the codification of the laws of Athens and the creation of the coherent legal system, and the reforms throughout the economy in both the agricultural and in the manufacturing sector were all designed to give every aspect of Athenian life a more formal and coherent basis. I would argue that it is that which is the first step towards the growth of Athenian democracy and the final efflorescence and brilliance of Athenian culture in the Classical age.

# Lecture Ten
# Tyranny

**Scope:**

The term "tyranny" conjures up images of cruel despots terrorizing a frightened population. In the world of ancient Greece, especially in the sixth century, tyranny meant something quite different. Tyrants were ambitious men who took advantage of the upheavals of the age to seize power. Some, like Policrates of Samos, were great builders. Many, like Cypselus of Corinth, ruled during a time of prosperity. By ending the factional disputes that afflicted the city-states of Greece, many of them brought stability.

The Athenians were ruled by the tyrant Pisistratus and his sons for half a century. Far from being a time of fear, this was a period during which the Athenians enjoyed peace at home and growing influence abroad. In this lecture we will examine the tyranny of Pisistratus and its legacy for Athens.

## Outline

I. After Solon.

    **A.** The period after Solon's departure from Athens (593 B.C.) saw no improvement in the bitter factional fighting that had afflicted the city.

        **1.** For two years the violence was so bad that no archon was elected, causing Athens to lapse into a period of literal anarchy.

        **2.** A leading politician named Damasias was elected and refused to give up office. He was expelled after two years.

    **B.** In the next generation, three factions emerged in Athenian politics: the Men of the Shore, the Men of the Plain, and the Men from Beyond the Hills.

        **1.** Each corresponded loosely to one of the regions of Attica.

        **2.** Each faction was dominated by aristocratic leaders.

        **3.** The leader of the Hill faction, from the eastern part of Attica, was Pisistratus.

**II.** Pisistratus made three attempts to establish himself as tyrant. The details of these attempts shed light on the weakness of the Athenian state.

**A.** In 561 Pisistratus made his first attempt to become tyrant.

**1.** Appearing in the marketplace disheveled and bruised, he claimed to have been attacked by his enemies.

**2.** Given permission to raise a bodyguard, he occupied the Acropolis, the citadel of Athens.

**3.** Shortly thereafter, he was driven out.

**B.** In 558 he made his second attempt at establishing a tyranny by means of a marriage alliance with another leading family.

**1.** His young wife complained that Pisistratus was uninterested in properly consummating the marriage.

**2.** They separated, the alliance ended, and Pisistratus withdrew from Athens to the region of Thrace, where he enriched himself by opening gold and silver mines.

**C.** In 546 Pisistratus returned to Athens richer, better equipped, and supported by the goddess Athena.

**1.** Accompanied by a six-foot-tall Athenian girl called Phye dressed as Athena, Pisistratus and a private army marched on Athens.

**2.** His opponents were defeated at the battle of Pallene, and Pisistratus finally became the tyrant of Athens.

**III.** Pisistratus' Accomplishments.

**A.** Fifty years after the expulsion of the last of Pisistratus' family, Herodotus investigated the tyranny and came to the conclusion that Pisistratus had ruled mildly, had obeyed the law, and had generally done a great deal to benefit the Athenians.

**B.** Some modern historians would go further and say that Pisistratus was actually more important for the establishment of democracy than Solon. Consider his record:

**1.** He maintained existing laws and allowed elections to take place every year.

**2.** He appointed rural magistrates so that poor farmers could get legal redress without having to quit their farms.

**3.** He embarked on a building program that included construction of a temple to Athena on the Acropolis, a fountain house in the market-place, and the temple of Olympian Zeus

4. He made loans to the poor at low interest.
5. He introduced a 10 percent tax on produce to give the Athenian state financial revenues.
6. He expanded the mining of silver at Laurium and in Thrace, helping to make Athens the center of a trading and mercantile realm that encompassed the Aegean.

**IV.** Pisistratus and the Creation of Athens.

**A.** Along with this impressive record, Pisistratus was responsible for the cultural transformation of Athens. Festivals such as the Dionysia and Panathenaia, which involved athletic and musical contests, made Athens into the preeminent cultural center of the Greek world.
1. Archaic sculpture in Athens reached a new level of excellence.
2. Attic Black-Figure vases now outstripped Corinthian pottery as a luxury item and were traded as far away as Etruria.

**B.** Pisistratus conducted an aggressive foreign policy that added to Athens' prosperity.
1. He conducted peaceful relations with other tyrants such as Lygdamis of Naxos and Policrates of Samos.
2. Under Pisistratus' leadership, the Athenians annexed the island of Delos, acquiring control of the prestigious sanctuary of Apollo.

**C.** The effect of all this was the creation of Athens.
1. Before Pisistratus, Athens consisted of warring clans competing for political power just as they competed in war and in Olympic competition.
2. Although Pisistratus was himself an ambitious aristocrat, he managed to bequeath to the Athenians a state that had a far more clearly defined sense of Athenian identity.

**D.** After the death of Pisistratus (528/7 B.C.), his sons continued to hold power, probably through alliances with some of the leading families. The sons, however, were not the equal of the father. In 514, one of Pisistratus' sons, Hipparchus, was assassinated, and four years later his brother, Hippias, was driven from the city.

**V.** The man who emerged from the next round of civil *stasis* would be the man who profited from Pisistratus' legacy, the man who would recognize that the common Athenian was a more potent political force than the most powerful aristocrat. His name was Cleisthenes, and it was he more than any other who finally established the Athenian democracy.

### Suggested Reading

Andrewes, A. (1956) *The Greek Tyrants*. London: Methuen.

### Questions to Consider

1. Was tyranny a necessary stage for the political development of the Greek states?
2. Was the Panathenaia the most important legacy of the Pisistratid tyranny?

# Lecture Ten—Transcript
## Tyranny

Welcome back to our tenth lecture in this series on Ancient Greek Civilization. In the last couple of lectures, we've been examining the Archaic period in Greek history. We've been looking at the way in which this was a period of great tension, turmoil and upheaval, even as it was also a period of great accomplishment, new wealth, new artistic styles and so forth.

We looked at Sparta in particular to see the way in which one community in Greece tried to deal with the tension of the period. We noted that in that case, the Spartans really took a very different tack from the rest of the communities of ancient Greece by closing in on themselves and keeping the rest of the Greek world at bay.

We saw when we turned our attention to Athens that there the attempt to deal with the *stasis*—the conflict—which bedeviled the affairs of the Greeks was to appoint a single man, Solon, as archon in 594 B.C. in an attempt to push through a set of reforms that would save Athens from collapsing into anarchy and then potentially tyranny.

This fear of tyranny is one of the features of the Archaic period that we come up against time and time again. Before we talk more about the actual instance of tyranny that we know best, that of Pisistratus in Athens, we have to be clear that we understand exactly what the term "tyranny" means. When we use the term, it tends to conjure up images of cruel despots who are terrorizing a frightened population, putting people to death, and ruling by fiat rather than by the rule of law.

In the world of ancient Greece, and especially in the sixth century B.C., tyranny really means something very different. It is a term borrowed by the Greeks from Lydia—*tyrannos*. Originally, a tyrant is quite simply someone who has reached supreme power but was not elected to it. In a way, it is a value-neutral term originally. A tyrant is not a king; he was not born to that power. He is not a president, archon or prime minister; he was not elected to that power. He is someone who has seized power.

In the world of the sixth century B.C., what this really means in practice is ambitious men who take advantage of the disorder and upheavals of the time to take power in their home city. Whether they're good men or bad men, whether they're successful rulers, or whether they're tyrannical in our sense of the word is not part of the original meaning of tyrant. It simply means that they have used the turmoil of the time to come to power and seize power themselves.

Some of them, in fact, were great builders like Policrates of Samos. You can still see, if you go to the island of Samos, the Eupalinos Tunnel, which he engineered running through the mountain to help bring water down to his city. Some of them ruled during periods of enormous prosperity for their city. For example, Corinth, which became one of the great trading powers of the Archaic period, was ruled through much of that period by the family of the Cypselidae, descendents of Cypselus, who is remembered for encouraging the prosperity of Corinth as a trading power at the time.

By ending the dreadful factional disputes which had afflicted the Greek city-states in the sixth century B.C., many of the tyrants actually brought a period of relative stability and harmony to their city-states. Their legacy is a complex one. They can't be regarded, as they used to be, as a block to the development of democracy. Often in fact, they actually encouraged the later development of democracy. We'll go into that later today.

The Athenians are our best-known example of a Greek state ruled by a tyrant. The tyrant Pisistratus and his sons ruled them for at least a half century—the second half of the sixth century B.C. This period in Athenian history, far from being a time of fear, arbitrary rule, secret police or autocracy, rather was a period during which the Athenians enjoyed peace at home and growing influence abroad and great prosperity.

In this lecture, I want to concentrate now on the family of Pisistratus and the tyranny experienced by the Athenians in the sixth century B.C. in an attempt to understand the importance of this to the subsequent course of Athenian history and culture.

You might remember that in our last lecture I pointed out that in the period after Solon, Athens actually saw not an improvement, but a worsening of the *stasis*—the civil conflict which had afflicted the state. For two years, as I mentioned, we had a period of literal anarchy—no archon being elected. For another two years, an individual by the name of Damasias tried to seize power and establish himself as tyrant.

During the next generation after this period of great turmoil in the late 590s, 580s and down into the 570s B.C., three factions would emerge dominating Athenian politics. They're labeled for us by Aristotle, who tells us that they were called the "Men of the Shore", the "Men of the Plain", and the "Men from Beyond the Hills". Quite clearly, these are regional markers. These factional names refer to the parts of the territory of Athens—Attica—that these different groups came from. We don't know a great deal about them, but from what we know, it seems as if each of these factions was ruled by an aristocratic leader. We have here a combination of that aristocratic factionalism that I've mentioned in the past and regional distinctions in the Athenian state as well.

The leader of the last of these factions, the Men from either the Hill or Beyond the Hill, was known as Pisistratus, and he's going to be the important character we deal with today. Pisistratus actually had to make three attempts at establishing himself as tyrant of Athens. I want to rehearse the details of those attempts, because not only are they interesting stories on their own, but I think they serve to remind us of how weak the power of the Athenian state was at this stage in its history. That's worth keeping in mind.

The three attempts at tyranny by Pisistratus: these begin in 561 B.C. On this occasion, Pisistratus appeared in the marketplace of Athens, the *agora*. He was disheveled. His clothes had been torn apart and he was bruised and scratched. He claimed that he had been attacked by his enemies in a factional fight, a typical example of *stasis*. He therefore requested that he be allowed to raise a bodyguard—club bearers. After he'd been given permission by the Athenians to do this, he promptly marched up to the Acropolis, installed himself there, and proclaimed himself tyrant. Shortly after, he was driven out.

It has always struck me that this episode seems vaguely absurd. This sounds more like little boys in first grade playing king of the castle. The very fact that this could be the way in which the affairs of the Athenians are worked out in the sixth century B.C. I think reminds us of just how weak the central authority of Athens is. Athens is up for grabs between these competing factions.

In 558 B.C., three years later, Pisistratus made his second attempt at establishing a tyranny and he did this by the much more legitimate means of establishing a marriage alliance between himself and the faction of another leading family. Unfortunately, according to our sources, his young wife complained to her family that Pisistratus was not interested in consummating the marriage properly. Exactly what that means, we can't be sure. It may be generous to interpret it that he already had sons from an earlier marriage and didn't wish to complicate matters by fathering new children. For whatever reason exactly, they then separated shortly after and the alliance between Pisistratus and the other faction broke down. As a result, Pisistratus withdrew from Athens, facing opposition from the other factions.

Upon withdrawing from Athens around 558 B.C., he moved north to the northern Aegean to the region of Thrace. He spent the best part of the next decade up there enriching himself as he opened new gold and silver mines. It was as a result of the wealth that he accumulated in the late 550s and early 540s B.C. that he then returned to Athens in 546 B.C.

This, his third attempt at establishing the tyranny, was in many ways the most remarkable attempt of all. Herodotus tells the story and says that the Athenians are normally regarded as the most intelligent of the Greeks, but this story does really not redound to their credit at all.

The story is that on this third occasion when Pisistratus returned, he landed in eastern Attica at Brauron, where his family regional base was located. There, he took a girl by the name of Phye, who was six feet tall. That may be unremarkable for us, but of course, it is exceptional for the Greeks of the sixth century B.C. He dressed her up as the goddess Athena with a suit of armor, put her in a chariot, and then proceeded in ceremonial fashion to drive from Brauron to the city of Athens, with the Athenians lining the way convinced that it was the goddess Athena herself who was escorting Pisistratus back to Athens.

That's the colorful story. The slightly more mundane historical detail that must be added is that his opponents did oppose this return. They brought him to battle and at the Battle of Pallene in 546 B.C., Pisistratus was able to defeat his enemies and finally, once and for all, to establish himself as the tyrant of Athens.

Notice, though, where is there an Athenian army? Where is there an Athenian state or government force opposing him and defending the state against him? It doesn't exist because Athens at this stage is still nothing really more than a combination of different factions fighting each other.

That's what it was at the beginning of Pisistratus' rule around 546 B.C. It was not that by the time of the end of the rule of the Pisistratans toward the end of the sixth century B.C.

I want to talk, then, about the transformation that took place in Athens as a result of Pisistratus being in power. A good place to begin is by going to Herodotus who, 50 years after the expulsion of the Pisistratan family, investigated the tyranny. He wanted to understand what impact it had had. He came to the somewhat remarkable conclusion that Pisistratus had in fact ruled very mildly, that he had essentially obeyed all the laws that had been handed down from Solon, and that in general, Pisistratus had done a great deal to benefit the Athenians.

Taking their cue from Herodotus, some modern historians would go even further. They would say that looked at over the long haul—over the whole expanse of Athenian history and democracy—Pisistratus may have been finally more important for the establishment of the democracy than even Solon.

Let's consider his record then to see whether these claims bear examination. First of all, we know that he maintains the existing body of law. This means that every year still the Athenians met and elected new magistrates. It is not as if government was suspended by Pisistratus. It's true, of course, that the majority of people being elected to these offices were probably members of Pisistratus' family or other factions that were allied to him. The net effect was to continue this sense of the regularity of Athenian government. In fact, probably most other great families came to some sort of accommodation with Pisistratus, so that what we end up with here is a more stable sharing of power between the great families of Athens, with Pisistratus acting as a kind of moderator over the whole affair.

Furthermore, he appointed rural magistrates, so the poor farmers could actually get legal redress out in the countryside. This also is an important step if you think about it. On the one hand, of course, it means they don't have to quit their farms and come into the city center, so it encourages people not to come into Athens and mill about and congregate, which some sources say he was afraid of because this might lead to unrest. More importantly, I think, it reinforces for every Athenian—not just the people living in downtown Athens, but for the farmers living 30 miles out of Athens—the notion that there is a rule of law guaranteed by the Athenian state which will protect them and give them a hearing. They don't have to travel into Athens for this; it will even come to them. That I think is an important development.

Another much more straightforward and material benefit is that he embarked upon an extremely ambitious building program. This included a temple to Athena up on the Acropolis. If you've been to the Acropolis, you'll of course have seen the Parthenon and the Erechtheion, but between the two of them, if you look at the bedrock, you will actually see the cut bedrock bearing the foundations of that temple built by the Pisistratans. The rest of the temple is now gone.

He built a fountain house down in the *agora*. That may not seem like anything particularly significant to us, but for an ancient community as it is growing larger and larger, the water supply is in fact quite an important issue. We get some measure of the importance of this by the fact that many vases from that century in this period show this very fountain house. In other words, it had an impact on people. They thought, "This man is actually benefiting downtown Athens." I'm sure that the Athenian women who had to find water every day and bring it back to their houses—there was no running water—were very thankful that Pisistratus had built this new fountain house in the *agora*.

He started on an ambitious new temple to Olympian Zeus. If you've been to Greece, you may have seen that there are a certain number of buildings that are unfinished. The Temple of Olympian Zeus, which was started in the sixth century B.C., was still unfinished in the second century A.D. when a Roman emperor tried to finish it off. Alas, it is still unfinished to this day. Nevertheless, he started on that project.

He made loans to the poor at a low rate of interest to try and encourage the growth of the economy. At the same time (like any good government official, if he gives with one hand, he takes away with the other), he also made sure that people were paying a 10 percent tax on produce. You may hear the word "tax" and your blood will curdle. Taxes are not very popular in this country or anywhere else for that matter, but think about it for a moment. Taxes are actually important for one thing: if you have no taxes, you have no state. The state to exist must have revenues. Its revenues are only raised from taxes. By creating a regular system of taxation on produce, he was giving the Athenian state a solid source of financial revenue.

In fact, he was probably responsible for an extraordinary growth in the revenues of Athens, because not only did he introduce this tax, he also vastly expanded the mining operations taking place on the soil of Athens. This was in southern Attica, down at a place called Laurion, where there was a very rich vein of silver, which the Athenians now began to mine and then mint vigorously. Also in Thrace, where his own wealth had accumulated, many Athenians moved into the area and acquired property. They did so for its natural resources, particularly for the precious metals that were to be found there.

The net effect of these changes, particularly the growth in the mining of silver, was to make Athens the center of a trading and mercantile realm that encompassed the Aegean. It's at this time that Athenian coinage will turn up in excavations not just in Athens, but around the entire Aegean. People are using Athenian coinage and the wealth of Athens as the commodity for the trade of the Aegean.

In all these ways, then, he contributed to the expansion of Athens and to the stability and harmony of Athens in the sixth century B.C. He was also responsible for quite an astonishing cultural transformation, which I think was to have deep effect on the Athenians. I want to talk about some of the details of that for a moment.

The Athenian civic year was tied to the Athenian agricultural year and to the Athenian religious year. Festivals, harvest events and so forth were all tied together. Part of this calendar was a set of festivals, including the *Dionysia* and the *Panathenaia*. At the festival in honor of Dionysus, dramatic contests would take place and musical contests as well. At the *Panathenaia*, similar contests would take place in honor of Athena. The very title of the *Panathenaia* gives you a conception of what its significance is. It is for "all Athens": the Panathenaia festival.

These festivals were greatly expanded under the influence of Pisistratus and his sons. As a result, festivals that originally had been small or insignificant local festivals, under the Pisistratans became major athletic and cultural contests that drew competitors and contestants from all over the Greek world. In many respects, the *Panathenaia*, in terms of its status, prestige, importance and the wealth that it gave to winners, was really equivalent in status to a panhellenic festival. You remember that we've already talked about the significance of those festivals for bringing together all of the Greeks. Under Pisistratus, an Athenian festival now assumed that status as well, bringing together Greeks from all over to compete athletically and culturally.

This was to have very great importance in a number of different ways. For example, the Homeric poems bear very strongly the mark of a period of development in Athens. This looks to be not part of the earlier epic tradition of the Dark Ages, but rather to date from the time when the Homeric poems were being performed on a regular basis in Athens at the Panathenaic festival. As a result of that, there are references to Athens that are put into the poems themselves.

We find Athens during the second half of the sixth century B.C. assuming quite an extraordinary status in the Greek world as an economic center and as a cultural center as well. This can be attested in a number of different genres and areas of the arts. For example, the sculpture of Athens in the Archaic period reaches quite an extraordinary new level of excellence. It really begins to outstrip sculpture from other parts of Greece.

Similarly, in the area of vase painting—we have to consider vases not only in terms of their own beauty, but also as markers of trade, since they are often transporting goods to another place—it is at this time that black figure vases from Attica or Athens begin to supplant Corinthian pottery as luxury items and were traded as far away as, for example, Italy. In the Etruscan tombs which were opened in the last 200 years, one finds very commonly black figure Attic vases. If the Etruscans are paying to have these in their tombs, it means that they regard them as luxury items. That means that there is a demand for this Attic pottery. It's becoming a high status item.

We have this cultural transformation. We have this being tied to an economic transformation as high quality Athenian goods are turning up far abroad and this consistently goes with quite a new aggressive foreign policy that could be tied to Athenian prosperity of the time as well. For example (this is perhaps not so remarkable), one finds that Pisistratus as the tyrant of Athens was interested in conducting friendly relations with the tyrants of other Greek states. We hear of the Athenians, for example, dealing with Lygdamis of Naxos and Policrates of Samos. These are members of a sort of mutual self-help society of the Greek tyrants of the sixth century B.C.

In addition to dealing internationally with other tyrants who like him were impressive builders and leaders, Pisistratus was responsible for the annexation of the island of Delos. This is quite a remarkable event. Delos is one of the great Greek sanctuaries. It is dedicated to the god Apollo, who in myth was believed to have been born on that island. His mother, Leto, had wandered around heavily pregnant looking for a place where she could actually give birth and the island of Delos had allowed her to do it there. As a result, the entire island was a religious sanctuary. No one could be born on the island and no one could die on the island lest it be polluted. As a religious sanctuary in the middle of the Aegean, it became both a popular site of pilgrimage and an important economic center as well—a neutral spot where traders could come from different parts of the Greek world. It was a very prestigious sanctuary, almost to the caliber of Olympia or Delphi.

Under Pisistratus, the Athenians took over control of the sanctuary. This, therefore, is a very potent statement for the power of Athens. Athens is declaring itself as the dominant power in the Aegean if it can control the island of Delos.

If we consider all of these changes together—the economic reforms, the foreign policy, the territorial annexation, the new wealth, the increasing trade, the building program, the reliance on the same body of law, the help for the small farmers, and so forth—what I think we get is more than just an increasing prosperity for Athens. I think we get the creation of Athens. By that, I mean that before Pisistratus, Athens had been nothing more than this agglomeration of towns and villages and regional clans locked into fighting with each other. These clans had been like the Homeric heroes that we read about. They had been like the Olympic competitors that we read about. They are locked into this same pattern of endless competition, strife and the *agon*, or the conflict.

Pisistratus had arisen from exactly that same milieu as well. We can't deny that. He also was an ambitious aristocrat who originated the same way as all these others. But by the sheer length of his reign and the sheer range of his legislation and his activity, what he managed to bequeath to the Athenians at the end of his reign was a much more clearly articulated sense of the Athenian identity and of the Athenian state. From now on in Greek affairs, and in the affairs particularly of the Athenians, there will be a strong sense of there being an Athenian state—a government, a rule of law and a regularity in all the affairs of the Athenians.

That, in fact, will be what makes possible the next major step, which will be democracy and the institutions of democracy. That would be a little while in coming, however.

Pisistratus died in about 528/527 B.C. After his death, his sons continued to rule after him. This is a very common feature of tyranny in the Greek world, where the sons try to establish something of a dynastic rule following the successful rule of their ambitious father. However, in the case of the sons of Pisistratus, particularly Hippias and Hipparchus, they were not the equals of their father and their rule collapsed shortly after.

In 514 B.C., one of Pisistratus' sons, Hipparchus, would be assassinated. It is probably that very late period of the tyranny between 514–510 B.C., the years after the assassination of Hipparchus and the expulsion of Hippias, that we find the tyranny turning as we would say tyrannical. That is to say that Hippias, after the death of his father and the murder of his brother, resorted to a much more autocratic style of rule until he eventually was driven out by the Athenians.

What would follow is what we will deal with in the next lecture. To set the groundwork for that, we have to recognize that with the death of Pisistratus, the death of Hipparchus and then the expulsion of Hippias, there would come yet another fresh round of civil *stasis* (civil warfare). The path toward democracy was never easy for the Athenians.

The man who would profit from Pisistratus' legacy and recognize that the common Athenian was in a way a more potent political force than any powerful aristocrat was the man who would really finally embark the Athenians on the road towards democracy. His name is Cleisthenes. He is in charge of the Athenian state in the years 510–508 B.C. and it is he, more than any other, who finally will establish the brilliance of the Athenian democracy.

# Lecture Eleven
# The Origins of Democracy

**Scope:**

Although Solon and Pisistratus paved the way for Athens to become a full democracy, it was the aristocratic leader Cleisthenes who devised the democratic system under which Athens flourished for two centuries. In this lecture we examine the conditions under which democracy came into being. We then look in detail at the complex system set in place by Cleisthenes. By creating new tribal and local divisions, he forever weakened the aristocratic hold on Athenian politics. We will review some of the major interpretations that have been advanced to explain the Cleisthenic system.

## Outline

I. The End of the Pisistratid Tyranny.

    **A.** Popular tradition maintained that two Athenian aristocrats—Harmodius and Aristogeiton—slew Hipparchus in 514 B.C. and ended the tyranny. In fact, Hippias continued to hold power for four more years.

    **B.** Certain leading Athenian families—especially the Alcmeonidae—claimed to have opposed the tyrants throughout their rule. This, too, is false. Epigraphic evidence discovered in 1939 demonstrates that supposed opponents of the tyrants were in Athens holding office in the 520s, in the midst of the period of tyrannical rule.

    **C.** It is likely that Hippias, the other son of Pisistratus, ruled with a heavy hand only in the years after his brother's assassination, in 514.

        **1.** Resistance to the tyranny began to solidify only during the regime of Hippias.

        **2.** In 510 Hippias was driven out by the Spartans.

II. The Ascendancy of Cleisthenes.

    **A.** Newly liberated, the Athenians faced the question of how to conduct their own affairs. At first, they returned to the same factional strife that had marked the period before the tyranny.

**B.** Two leaders emerged in 510: Isagoras and Cleisthenes.
  1. As tension increased, Isagoras called for the banishment of Cleisthenes and his clan.
  2. Isagoras also called on the Spartans to assist him, but the Athenians resisted this external interference and rose up against the Spartan force led by Cleomenes. The Spartans were allowed to withdraw, and Isagoras went into exile with them.

**C.** Cleisthenes' success was due to the fact that he had proposed a popular plan to reform the Athenian constitution.
  1. Cleisthenes was a demagogue who appealed directly to the people.
  2. Herodotus says that Cleisthenes took "the people into his political club," which suggests that Cleisthenes promised the whole Athenian population a more direct voice in political affairs.

**D.** The plan called for redrawing the political map of Attica.
  1. Four existing tribes were replaced by ten new tribes (*phylae*).
  2. Each tribe was divided into three thirds (*trittyes*).
  3. Each of these thirds was located in one of the three regions of Attica: coast, inland, and city.
  4. Each third was composed of a varying number of demes, i.e., villages or municipalities, of which there were a total of 140. These demes varied widely in size.

**E.** Cleisthenes also created a Council of 500 to supervise and prepare the work of the popular Assembly.
  1. The composition of the Council changed every year.
  2. Each tribe supplied 50 councillors who served for one month.
  3. Each deme was allocated a quota of council positions which it filled by lot each year.
  4. In this way, every Athenian was likely to serve on the Council at least once, and usually not more than once, in his lifetime.

**F.** The reforms were intended to break the dominance of the old aristocratic clans and spread power as widely as possible throughout Athenian society. Both the tribal reform and the composition of the new Council reflect important principles that remained central to the democracy:

1. The annual rotation of power.
2. The sharing of power.
3. The preferability of sortition (choice by lot).

**III.** The Cleisthenic system looks and is complicated. Historians are compelled to ask, what plan lies behind this? Who profited from it? There are three main theories:

   **A.** Military Levies.
  1. Many scholars note that Cleisthenes' reorganization of the political boundaries of Attica has military implications. Athenians fought in tribal regiments; their officers were elected as tribal officers; and so, the argument goes, the Cleisthenic system resulted in a more regular, reliable muster.
  2. Yet this seems to confuse results with intention. The division of the army into ten tribal units hardly requires or explains the extraordinary complexity of the Cleisthenic system.

   **B.** A second theory is that Cleisthenes, an Alcmeonid, designed an elaborate system to spread the influence of the Alcmeonid family over three separate tribes.
  1. The theory is based on extremely suspect evidence concerning the deme affiliations of the Alcmeonidae.
  2. Nor is it clear that spreading the family's members across three tribes would mean three times as much influence. It may have had the opposite effect—i.e., diluting the family's influence.

   **C.** The third argument is that Cleisthenes' plan was to break the political power of the old, regionally based clans. By mixing up different demes in a Trittyes, breaking old ties, and connecting trittyes from different parts of the state, he was making it harder for old families to organize their supporters into a coherent political faction.

**IV.** The Result.

   **A.** The democracy, therefore, was not simply created by chance, nor did it involve the simple shedding of aristocratic influence. It required something both more dramatic and complicated, a revolutionary new order in which every man could be proud of his birth and proud of his citizenship.

**B.** If you asked an Athenian of the democracy his name, he replied in three parts: his given name, his father's name, and the name of his Cleisthenic deme. The Athenians were now forced to identify themselves by their place, literally, in the democracy.

## Suggested Reading

Eliot, C.W.J. (1962) *Coastal Demes of Attika: A Study of the Policy of Kleisthenes.* Toronto: University of Toronto Press.

Bicknell, P.J. (1972) *"Kleisthenes as Politician: An Exploration,"* in Studies in Athenian Politics and Genealogy (= Historia Einzelschriften Heft 19).

## Questions to Consider

1. Is it necessary to look for a partisan motive behind the reforms of Cleisthenes?
2. How important for the emergence of a full democracy was the creation of the Council of 500?

# Lecture Eleven—Transcript
## The Origins of Democracy

Welcome back to this, our eleventh lecture in a series on Ancient Greek Civilization. Today, we're going to be looking more closely at the origins of democracy.

In the last two lectures, we've dealt with two of the reformers and statesmen of the sixth century B.C. who had an enormous impact on the development of democracy in ancient Athens. We first looked at Solon, whose archonship in 594 B.C. saw a series of reforms that had long reaching effects on Athenian and Greek life. I pointed out that he had been elected as an economic reformer and that in the *Seisachtheia*, or "shaking off of debts" or "shaking off of burdens," he had instituted a series of economic reforms. I pointed out that he also had instituted constitutional reforms by creating four census classes by which the Athenian state would now be organized and which would give people access to various levels of participation in government.

We did notice that in the reforms of Solon, the short-term effect was not particularly beneficial because Athens remained mired in *stasis*, this rivalry and conflict between factions that we've seen occurring in Greek history.

We saw then that the second great figure of the sixth century B.C. was Pisistratus. Though he was not a constitutional reformer—in fact he was quite the opposite, in that he was in fact a tyrant who had seized power illegally—we saw that nevertheless he had an immense impact on the development of Athens, primarily by helping to more clearly articulate a sense of Athenian identity and commonality, if you will.

We saw this through the reforms he instituted economically that led to a much greater degree of prosperity in Athens. We saw a cultural transformation of Athens so that what in the 560s B.C. had been a city-state afflicted by *stasis* and the conflict of various rival groups, by the end of the decade was now proclaiming itself and seeing itself as one of the most powerful Greek city-states not only of the mainland, but also of the entire Aegean basin.

If we turn then to the end of the tyranny and see what follows from here, we find something extremely interesting. In the century or so after tyranny collapsed at Athens, the Athenians in their newly established democracy tried to suggest to themselves that in fact the tyranny had been a terrible period and that most of them had opposed it all along. What we're going to find in the period after the end of the tyranny in Athens is that there is a great deal of imaginative reconstruction of what went on in the period before.

Let me illustrate that with a concrete example that's worth knowing about. The popular tradition in Athens in the fifth century B.C. was that two Athenian aristocrats had slain the tyrant and had set Athens on the road to democracy. In fact, this was recalled even in a drinking song that Athenian men would sing while they were drinking at their evening dinner parties. In this song, one of the singers holds up his cup and says, "I toast Harmodius and Aristogeiton who slew the tyrants and made Athens a place of equal law (*isonomia*)."

That memory is completely wrong. The tyranny did not collapse with the slaughter of Hipparchus in 514 B.C. It actually continued for another four years.

Before we go on, I don't want to simply point out a misconception in the minds of Athenians, but I want to try to explain how that could come about and what use it served. For that, I need to explain the story of Harmodius and Aristogeiton a little bit more fully. This drinking song that I've referred to recalls the death of Hipparchus. The circumstances of that death are as follows. In 514 B.C., Hipparchus, the younger son of the tyrant Pisistratus, by now dead, had fallen in love with a young Athenian aristocrat by the name of Aristogeiton. He had made advances toward Aristogeiton but he was rebuffed. Aristogeiton was already in a relationship with another older Athenian man named Harmodius.

Having been rebuffed, Hipparchus decided to take vengeance. The way he did this was by having dismissed from an important parade in Athens, the Panathenaic festival, the sister of Aristogeiton, who had been scheduled to carry a basket and have an important role in this ceremony in honor of Athena. Faced with this slight, Aristogeiton and Harmodius, his older lover, came to the Panathenaic procession armed and, coming upon Hipparchus at one end of the procession on the outskirts of Athens as he was preparing the various participants to begin the procession into town, they slew the tyrant. They were quickly caught and killed.

As we know, Hippias continued to rule for another four years afterwards, but there was something about this story that caught the imagination of the Athenians. I think what it unfortunately represents is that a good sex scandal will probably last a lot longer in people's imagination than solid history. People were quite happily believing, 50 years after the event, that the tyranny had ended on that day, when in fact, all the solid evidence was that it had continued at least for another four years.

This myth making about the end of the tyranny is actually quite an important point. Let me illustrate further. Most of the leading families of Athens at later times maintained that during the tyranny they had remained opposed to the tyrant. One leading family, the family of the Alcmaeonids, one of the most powerful families in Athenian history, even went so far as to claim that during all the years of the tyranny, they had withdrawn voluntarily from Athens: they would not live in the city while it was being ruled by the tyrant Pisistratus and his sons.

We had no reason to disbelieve that until 1939, when an American archaeologist, excavator and epigrapher by the name of Benjamin Meritt came upon a very small piece of marble in the Athenian *agora* which he was able to demonstrate was in fact a list of the archons of the late sixth century B.C. There, smack bang in the middle of the 520s B.C.—at the very height of the Pisistratan tyranny—was the name of one of the clan leaders of the Alcmaeonids, the family that had supposedly been in voluntary exile the whole time. This was good, solid, concrete—or I should probably say marble—proof that the whole tradition that the Alcmaeonids had been out of Athens during the tyranny in heroic exile was in fact not true. It was a later construct.

It's no wonder then that the Athenians had such mixed ideas and conflicting beliefs about the tyranny. I've made the argument, in fact, that the tyranny was quite a good period as far as the Athenians were concerned, and that it was a period of great prosperity.

After the death of Hipparchus, the remaining son of Pisistratus, Hippias, did become more tyrannical—more autocratic in his rule. As a result, it was in that final four years that resistance to the tyranny began to solidify. In fact, then, in 510 B.C., at the bidding of the Delphic Oracle—once again, we see the importance of Delphi in helping to shape the affairs of the Greeks—the Spartans marched into Athens and helped to expel Hippias the tyrant.

We face an absolutely critical moment here in the history of Athens. What will happen now at this moment, when in 510 B.C., after half a century, the Athenians finally find themselves once again liberated and in control of their own future? They're free to conduct their own affairs. The answer, depressingly, is they immediately slipped back into the same pattern of *stasis* and conflict that they had been suffering throughout the entire century.

In this return to factional strife, two new leaders emerged as the most powerful in Athenian politics in 510 B.C.: Isagoras and Cleisthenes. As tension increased between the two clans or factions, Isagoras began calling for the expulsion of Cleisthenes and his Alcmeonid clansmen on the grounds that they were under a curse from the god for a much earlier infraction long forgotten by most other people. Isagoras went so far as to call upon the Spartans to assist him. It had worked once; let's try it again.

At this moment, around 510 B.C., when Isagoras calls upon the Spartans to assist him, we find an event which I think marks an extraordinarily significant step forward for the Athenians. Remember the three attempts by Pisistratus to establish his tyranny, where we'd seen how weak the central authority of Athens was and how easily he had established himself? On this occasion, now 50 years later, when the Spartans were called in, the Athenians rose up against them. They resisted this invasion by the Spartans and resisted having their affairs dictated for them by this exterior power.

The Spartan force, sent under King Cleomenes, was actually bottled up on the Acropolis and was forced to agree to a treaty whereby it would withdraw from Athens. With them went into exile Isagoras. Cleisthenes was triumphant.

I believe it is not only the transformation of Athens under the tyranny that had set the stage for this. There was something else as well, and that is the appeal of Cleisthenes to the Athenians. Here we face some problems of chronology. We're not entirely sure at exactly what moment he made his proposals to the Athenians, but I think we have to imagine that the Athenian uprising against the Spartans was partly prompted by the fact that they had been promised a program of political reform by Cleisthenes. It was a popular program, and they had thrown their support behind it wholeheartedly. In other words, Cleisthenes was a demagogue: a man who was appealing directly to the people.

Herodotus refers to this in a phrase which is an extremely memorable one. He says that Cleisthenes' success was due to the fact that he took "the people into his political club." What does that mean? What does an expression like that really mean? The "political clubs" to which Herodotus is referring are called *hetaireia* in Greek. A single *hetaireia* is a loose clique, if you will, made up of men who have not paid fees to a party. They have not signed on to a particular platform. Rather, it is an informal grouping of men who, by virtue of friendly relations and perhaps marriage relations between their families, have agreed to work together for their mutual benefit politically. "You support my program or stand on this position, and I'll support you as well. I'll be there in court when you're on trial and I'll make sure that I vote on your behalf."

These small informal groups were obviously the creation of the factions and clans that had been part of Athenian politics for so long. If you think about it, there is no way literally that you can take the people—the whole population, the *demos*—into your political club. Technically and literally, it can't happen. I think what it must mean figuratively is that, for the first time, an Athenian, rather than thinking, "Who should I get my ally to be? What deal can I make with that leader over there? How can I position my clan in relation to that clan?" instead had recognized that there was a great untapped power if you could appeal directly to all of the Athenian population. If you could propose a program that would appeal to them and that they would support, then in a sense your *hetaireia* (political club) became not just your little clique of friends, it became all of the Athenian population.

That's only possible if you are aware of an Athenian population that is politically motivated, active and willing to participate in politics. That is the situation in 510 B.C.

He appealed as a demagogue to the Athenians. They threw their weight behind him and then, in 509–508 B.C., after the expulsion of Isagoras and the departure of the Spartans, Cleisthenes put into place a program of reform the like of which has never been seen in Greek history. In some respects, I've been suggesting to you the gradual growth of the Athenian democracy, but in other respects, the

Athenian democracy was born complete and full, like Athena springing out of the head of Zeus already fully formed. This is the moment at which it happens.

It is a very complicated system, but I want to explain it in quite close detail, so that you'll grasp exactly how the Athenian democracy originates and exactly how it operates. Here we go with something very detailed: the plans of Cleisthenes. Cleisthenes' plans relied upon completely redrawing all the political boundaries of Attica, Attica being the territory of Athens. Before this there had been four tribes and every member of the Athenian citizen body had been a member of one of those tribes. These were now replaced by 10 completely new tribes. They were given the names of various great heroes from the Athenian past, but no one had any illusions about these tribes being ancient and antique. They were created at one moment in Athenian history.

These 10 tribes were then each divided into three thirds—the so-called "*trittyes.*" These three thirds for each tribe were drawn from the various regions of Attica, so that each tribe would have one-third that came from the inland area, another third that was drawn from the coastal area, and it would have a third third that would come from the city. In other words, the population of any given tribe already included people from all different regions of Attica.

Each of these various thirds was itself made up of smaller units within its territory known as *demes*. These *demes* might be villages or they might be large towns. They varied in size from small villages to very large municipalities. There was a total of 140 of these. The actual number of *demes* in each third varies, but the idea seems to have been to have something like an equal population in each of the thirds by clustering together different *demes*.

I'll talk about the significance of this and what it means in a moment, but let me go forward for a moment and talk about more of the reforms of Cleisthenes. He also created a new Council of 500. This Council of 500 was there to supervise the work of the assembly, to draw up its agenda, and to make recommendations. It played a very important role in the day-to-day running of the democracy. This Council of 500 was a new creation and its creation depends upon the 10 tribes. Why? Because the 10 tribes each contributed a contingent of 50 men to the Council. We say a Council of 500, but a slightly more accurate description would be a Council of 10 times 50: 10 tribal units of 50 men.

The Athenian civic year was divided into 10 months. For one month of the year, one of these groups of 50 would be serving as the council and taking care of the affairs of the democracy. How was this Council selected? It was selected by giving each of the *demes* a quota: saying to each of the *demes,* "You must produce a certain number of counselors every year." The demes elect their counselors. These are then drawn together into the *trittyes* and into the tribe. This contingent of 50 serves for one month of the Athenian 10-month year.

The effect of this system is to create a Council which is not dominated by the great aristocratic clan leaders at all. Rather, it is one that represents a broad cross-section of the Athenian community. It means, because of this system, that virtually every man is going to serve on the Council, because once you've served, then you are not eligible for another 10 years. Every year there are people serving from all over Athens and then they're knocked out of the pool for the next year. A fresh batch has to be found.

The system depends upon a principle of the annual rotation of power. New people every year: new people in the magistracies, new people on the Council every year. Furthermore, it relies on this principle: the sharing of power. You don't have a single counselor, but rather you have 50 of them from a tribe. Then they move on quickly and are replaced by another 50. By this rotation and sharing of power, you manage to spread the power more evenly through all of Athens.

For some of these positions, rather than voting for nominated candidates, you simply take those who are eligible, put their names into a hat and pull out the winners. This is election by sortition—by lot—rather than election.

What does this all mean all put together? It means we've had a sudden overhaul of the Athenian political system. What we've had put into place very quickly and very firmly is a set of principles of sortition, rotation, annuality, and power sharing, all of which are designed to spread power through as many sectors of Athenian society as possible. This breaks the power of the old clan leaders and the old aristocrats, who have been running the affairs of Athens for the last century.

The program that I've just outlined sounds very complicated. The simple reason for that is it is very complicated. It's extraordinarily complicated. That such a complex system was initiated at a single moment in history—not developed over years, but put into place at one moment—has led historians to ask, "What on earth was Cleisthenes thinking? What is the planning that lies behind this?"

There have been actually very conflicting interpretations of the Cleisthenic reforms. What I want to do now is to give you those three interpretations and tell you what I think is perhaps the correct one. We might begin by posing the question that Roman lawyers used to pose: "*Que bono* (who profits) by the system?"

A number of scholars have pointed out that a great benefit of the system instituted by Cleisthenes is that it regularizes the raising of an Athenian army. The Athenian army is raised by tribal contingence. If you create these 10 tribes that incorporate every one in Athens, you have a very well organized muster whereby at a moment's notice all of the available men in Athens can be enlisted—put into the field. The regiments work that way. The officers are selected on a tribal basis and so forth.

So this is the military argument: that the Cleisthenic reforms are designed to create a more regular and more reliable muster. The difficulty that I have with this particular theory is that it runs the risk, in my opinion, of confusing the results of the Cleisthenic reforms with the intentions of the Cleisthenic reforms. Yes, it did result in a more reliable muster and an extremely efficient Athenian army that fought very well and successfully hereafter. Whether that was what Cleisthenes had in mind as he began the reforms—if that is what he was planning to begin with—we can't say. I don't think that such an explanation, for example, would explain the extreme complexity of the Cleisthenic reforms.

Let me illustrate this with an example. In one of the tribes created by Cleisthenes, its coastal third lies in the northeast of Attica. In that region, there are four villages that go together. They're located near each other. They sent a religious embassy to Delphi every year. They clearly thought of themselves as being a small corporation—four villages that were closely affiliated. In the Cleisthenic reforms, three of these stayed together as part of the third of one tribe; one of them was cut off and attached to a completely separate tribe. I don't see what sense that makes if your concern is with raising military musters. It would make more sense, in fact, to keep with the existing units that were already in place on the ground.

A second theory that is often used to explain the Cleisthenic reforms is an interesting theory. It's the ancient version of a conspiracy theory. Cleisthenes was a member of the Alcmeonid family. According to some historians, the reforms of Cleisthenes were designed to increase the influence and power of the Alcmeonid clan in Athenian politics.

How on earth can we know this? The way the argument is built is as follows: if you look at every reference that we have to an Alcmeonid in subsequent history and find out what *deme* he came from, since we can allocate *demes* to thirds and thirds to tribes, we can then say that this man's family was located in such and such a tribe. If you do this with the Alcmaeonids, based on some evidence which is not as firm as we might like it to be, it looks as if the Alcmaeonids as a clan or blood-related family were scattered across three different tribes in the Athenian democracy. "Aha!" say the conspiracy theorists. "This tends to demonstrate then that Cleisthenes was attempting to insinuate Alcmeonid influence across three tribes and therefore to make the Alcmaeonids three times more powerful. Instead of being powerful in one tribe, they were powerful in three."

There's a fairly obvious weakness in that interpretation as well. That is this: if you take a given clan—relatives, cousins, uncles, and nephews who are all willing to help each other and operate together—and spread their influence across three tribes, you may in fact be diluting their influence in the broader democracy. You will be reducing the numbers of that family in any given tribe. It's not at all clear that the Cleisthenic reforms would have benefited his own family. That's not demonstrable in later history and it doesn't particularly make sense with the evidence as it stands.

I don't believe that the Cleisthenic reforms were primarily to change the Athenian army, nor were they designed to make his family the Kennedys of the Greek world, as they've sometimes been likened to—a powerful family with a strong power base in one region. I think there's something else going on here. This goes back to certain themes that we've been talking about in the lectures so far. In my opinion, the correct interpretation of the Cleisthenic reforms is that he was intending to break the power of the old regionally based clans.

The Peisistratids were known to come from eastern Attica from the region of Brauron. In all the different parts of Attica, wherever you went, you would find powerful families who owned a certain amount of land, but who also counted among their supporters villagers from various other nearby areas. It is that sense of regionalism—of the connection between regions and clans—that had been the root source of *stasis* in Athens for a hundred years. It is that which I believe Cleisthenes was attempting to address.

I'll see if I can support that with another piece of evidence. You remember that I mentioned a minute ago a set of villages in the northeast of Attica which were all together a single religious corporation. By breaking off one of these four and putting it in a tribe which is actually located nowhere nearby—the other *demes* it's connected to do not border on it at all—what Cleisthenes was doing was making it impossible for those four villages—that region—to retain its importance in Athenian politics. Think about it for a minute: the men of that fourth village no longer sat in assembly with the men from the other villages. The men of that village were now incorporated into a whole other tribe. They served in a whole other tribal contingent. They sat in the assembly in a whole other tribal contingent.

Anyone who could dominate those four villages, that old corporation, might still be influential as a religious figure and might have some status, but could not call upon them as a block voting unit politically.

I might point out that Cleisthenes allowed those four villages to remain a religious corporation. It's just that that regional religious function no longer carried over into Athenian affairs at all.

He connected instead thirds from widely divergent regions, so that the voice of the Men from the Hill and the voice of the Men from the Shore would be heard in every tribe. Every tribe would mix up these units. Correspondingly, no regional group could ever then truly dominate, because its influence was spread across all of the various tribes.

This is really something very dramatic. If we think of the clans as being the expression of the kind of aristocratic culture that we noticed coming out of the Dark Ages and dominating in the Archaic period, then I think what we have with Cleisthenes is the first major concerted attempt to completely reorient the affairs of the Greeks and to destroy that old aristocratic culture.

The attempt would not be entirely successful. Leading families would still retain their status and their prestige. This happens even today in democracies. Nevertheless, it is true that by making it harder for the old aristocratic clans to dominate affairs, what Cleisthenes was doing was making it correspondingly easier for ordinary Athenians—for the *demos*—not to just be a part of his *hetaireia* (his political club), but to be the actual fundamental driving force of the democracy. These reforms make the democracy possible.

The Athenian democracy was not created just by chance and it didn't simply evolve slowly over the years. Rather it required at one moment in its history a determined attempt to break aristocratic influence and to replace that with something new. This was dramatic, it was complicated, but finally it was successful. The measure of it is this: in the Athenian democracy and in the Athenian culture of the fifth and fourth centuries B.C. if you asked an Athenian his name, he replied with three names: his own name, the name of his father and the name of his *deme*, his demotic. What Cleisthenes did was quite simply to give every Athenian a place in the democracy of ancient Athens.

# Lecture Twelve
# Beyond Greece—The Persian Empire

**Scope:**

Throughout the Archaic period, contact between Greeks and non-Greeks occurred as a result of trade and colonization. By the late sixth century, however, the Persian Empire had grown so vast and powerful that the Greeks of the Ionian Coast came into direct contact with the Persians, in some cases even becoming tributary states to the Persians. This set the stage for the epic confrontation between Persia and the Greeks which would change Greek history forever.

In this lecture, we will look at the Persian Empire, its origins under Cyrus the Great, and its territorial expansion. We will discuss the accomplishments of the Persians, attempting to avoid the bias of the Greek sources. What emerges is a great and sophisticated society, which, by historical accident, became a negative image of the Greeks' view of themselves.

## Outline

I. The Origins and Development of the Persian Empire.

    **A.** From the fourth millennium before Christ onwards, Mesopotamia (the region of modern Iraq) produced a succession of complex civilizations, including Sumer, Akkad, and the Assyrians. Cycles of growth, invasion, destruction, and regeneration followed each other for two thousand years.

    **B.** The Persians came from the periphery of this cultural zone.

        **1.** Their language was Indo-European, unlike the Semitic languages of Mesopotamia.

        **2.** Originally semi-nomadic, they came out of the great open steppes of southern Russia. Mesopotamia was neither their origin nor the heartland of their eventual empire.

        **3.** They settled in the high Iranian plateau early in the first millennium B.C., and they achieved political unification only in c. 700 B.C.

**C.** In 558 B.C. Cyrus the Great came to the throne. Soon he established the basis of the Persian Empire by conquering the Medes, a neighboring people. From here he continued the aggressive expansion of Persian power east and west.

    **1.** With the conquest of Babylon, Cyrus transformed the Persians from outsiders into the greatest imperial power of the ancient Near East.

    **2.** At the time of his death in 530, the Persian domain reached from Afghanistan to the Ionian coast.

**II.** Territorial Expansion Under the Achaemenid Dynasty.

**A.** Cyrus' conquests brought the Greeks of Asia Minor into direct contact with Persian power. With the conquest of Lydia, Persian control extended virtually to the Aegean.

    **1.** As illustrated by Herodotus, many Greeks sought to derive moral lessons from the rise of Persian power.

    **2.** Asia Minor was divided into a series of *satrapies* or provinces, often corresponding to the territory of the various pre-Persian kingdoms.

    **3.** The Persian King usually assigned the *satrapy* to a friend or relative. These governors, or *satraps*, enjoyed a great deal of independence.

**B.** Cyrus was succeeded by Cambyses (530–522), much of whose reign was taken up with the conquest of Egypt.

**C.** After the death of Cambyses, Darius came to the throne.

    **1.** According to Herodotus, the death of Cambyses was followed by a constitutional debate over possible new forms of government for the Persian Empire. This debate among various regimes—aristocracy, democracy, and monarchy—was more relevant to fifth-century Greece than to sixth-century Persia.

    **2.** Darius renewed the western expansion of the Persians. By c. 514, the Persians had reached the islands of the Aegean.

    **3.** The Greek cities along the Ionian coast came under Persian control.

    **4.** The Persians were generally content to leave the cities under the control of a cooperative tyrant.

    **5.** Persian rule was, for the most part, neither cruel nor onerous.

**D.** The final confrontation of Persia and Greece, in 490 and 480–79 B.C., should be seen as the culmination of Persian territorial expansion.

**E.** The idea that the wars represented a grand cultural clash between East and West emerged in fifth-century hindsight. At the time, the Greeks and Persians did not view their systems as antithetical.

    **1.** In the sixth-century context, the Greeks were insignificant vis-à-vis the Persians in terms of territory, empire, and power.

    **2.** Many Greeks lived and worked in the Persian empire and did not view the Persians as alien.

    **3.** At the time, few if any Greeks thought that Greece and Persia were bound inevitably to clash.

**III.** Iranian Culture and Society under the Achaemenids.

**A.** The Achaemenids favored the traditional Persian religion centered on the worship of the elements and natural forces, principally the sky, sun, moon, earth, fire and water. The Achaemenid kings especially honored the great Sky God, Ahura-Mazda, with whose authority they identified their own.

**B.** The Achaemenids were also tolerant of other religious systems. A letter of Darius to one of his *satraps* threatens him with punishment for cutting down trees sacred to Apollo.

**C.** Persian society was hierarchical.

    **1.** This was demonstrated by the act of obeisance, performed before a superior. Equals were greeted with a kiss.

    **2.** The King's friends and relatives constituted the ruling class. This mixed, Persian-Median aristocracy ruled over an empire that embraced tribes and peoples that differed greatly in speech, culture and manners.

    **3.** An imperial post and a system of roads crossing the empire created the finest communications network of the ancient world.

**D.** Military prowess was highly prized, with hunting and archery considered the proper training for warriors.

   **1.** Major military expeditions drew on contingents from all over the empire: the Phoenician fleet, horsemen from the Steppes, Greek and Carian heavy infantry, Assyrian chariots.

   **2.** Commanders invariably came from the ranks of the King's Friends.

**E.** The quality and refinement of Achaemenid jewelry, especially in gold, recalls something of the Persians' nomadic origins. At the same time, Achaemenid art synthesizes earlier Iranian traditions with the styles and techniques of the areas conquered. The Persians borrowed freely, and they employed artisans from all over their empire. Many Greeks, for example, from Ionia served as doctors, engineers and masons in the Persian royal city of Susa.

**F.** Before the Achaemenid kings the Persians had virtually no tradition of monumental architecture. Under the Achaemenids, however, extraordinary palaces at Persepolis and Susa were built to express the majesty of this ambitious people. The Persians bring together much that is best in the long cultural development in the ancient Near East.

## Suggested Reading

Cook, J.M. (1983) *The Persian Empire*. London.

## Questions to Consider

**1.** To what degree has understanding of the Persian Empire been skewed by our reliance on Greek literary sources?

**2.** What elements in Greek and Persian culture contributed most to the confrontation which resulted in the Persian Wars?

# Lecture Twelve—Transcript
## Beyond Greece—The Persian Empire

Welcome back to this, the twelfth of our lectures in a series on Ancient Greek Civilization and Greek History. In the course of the last 11 lectures, we've been charting the development of Greek civilization through the Bronze Age, then into the Iron Age, and now down very close to the Classical period. During that time, we've seen there have been moments in the history of the Greeks, as in the course of any culture, when that history will have abrupt changes. There will be moments when the cultural flow which has been developing for hundreds of years will change direction very quickly.

We're now reaching such a moment again in the history of the Greeks at the end of the sixth century B.C. During the Archaic period, we have seen the tension within the Greek world. We have seen the *stasis* in the various Greek communities. We have seen the different ways in which Greek states have tried to handle this, with Sparta closing down and becoming a rigidly fixed society, and Athens, on the other hand, exploring much more nuanced ways of dealing with this in the reforms of Solon, then seeing 50 years of Pisistratan tyranny, which truly transformed the Athenians, and then finally the triumphant career of Cleisthenes and the reforms of 510–508 B.C.

That nice development that we see going on through the sixth century, which begins in anarchy and ends in democracy, will now abruptly change. The incident or event which will mark a completely new direction in the history of the Greeks will be the Persian Wars. Because that is going to be so monumental an experience for the Greeks, today what I want to do is to set the stage for looking at the Persian Wars by looking at the Persian Empire. I want to see who these Persians were that the Greeks would be coming up against in 490 and 480–479 B.C.

As we do this, I want to do a second thing as well: not just to tell the story of the Persians, but to try to bring out the way in which what we know about the Persians, we tend to see through a Greek filter. It's not simply that we are trying to understand one culture through the lens of another culture, but that we are seeing the Persians from the point of view of the Greeks who, of course, fought against them in 490 and 480–479 B.C. and who defeated them. The impact of that victory, which we will see in another lecture, was of immense importance to the Greeks and is going to have an effect on how subsequently the Greeks write about the Persians and then from there, how we read and understand the Persians.

We have two focuses today: trying to understand the Persians and trying to see something of the way that the Greeks thought about them, and how these points of view took shape.

First of all, let's go back and talk about the origins of the Persians and try to find out how it should be that these people should end up in conflict with the world of the Greeks. The Persians, really, come from an entire milieu in the ancient Near East that has seen a succession of great civilizations. From the fourth millennium B.C. onwards, Mesopotamia, which is to say modern day Iraq, has been the homeland of a succession of complex cultures and civilizations: Sumer, Akkad, the power of Babylon, and later the Assyrians as well. Throughout these millennia, in this area of what is modern day Iraq, we've seen civilizations come and go. Civilizations rise and fall, to be replaced by new ones. This endless pattern of invasion, destruction and regeneration has gone on for thousands of years.

Most of the cultures of those millennia that succeeded each other, swallowed each other up, and then reproduced new power were cultures that were Semitic. Their languages are generally Semitic, related to Hebrew and Arabic today. Generally speaking, the focus and location of their power was always that area between the two fertile rivers, the Tigris and the Euphrates, the area the Greeks knew as "Mesopotamia" ("the land between the rivers").

The Persians are somewhat outside that cultural flow which has poured over the ancient Near East for millennia. For a start, their language was Indo-European. In other words, their language is in the same general family group that includes Greek. It includes Sanskrit at the other end. It goes in both directions, to India and also to Europe. Of course, it then includes our language, English, and German and French and so forth. We might like to recall this. Sometimes people forget that the Iranians today, the modern descendants of those Persians, are not Arabs. They are not Semitic speakers. They speak a language that is related to ours.

Secondly, not only are they outside of this flow of the cultures of the ancient Near East in being Indo-European and not Semitic, but they don't come from Mesopotamia and finally that is not really the heartland of their empire when they do become a great Near Eastern empire. They originally come from the southern steppes, from southern Russia. It is out of these great open steppes that these herdsmen and horsemen make their way sometime around 1000 B.C. This is obviously a very general date.

As they pour south into the high Iranian plateau, they remain scattered in separate tribes and groups of herdsmen, hunters and riders. It's not until about 700 B.C. that they become politically unified. Even then, they're still relatively weak and they're still on the outer side of that heartland of the ancient Near East of Mesopotamia.

This will change drastically in 558 B.C. (we're now getting to that stage of history when I can give you actual dates, which makes me very happy, compared to talking only about millennia). In 558 B.C., Cyrus the Great comes to the throne. He soon establishes very quickly the basis of Persian power—the Persian Empire—by conquering the neighboring tribe of the Medes. In doing so, he sets off a campaign of aggressive territorial expansion, which will lead into the growth of Persian power across the whole ancient Near East, eventually culminating of course in their conflict with the Greeks at the beginning of the fifth century B.C.

Cyrus the Great's reign, which lasts from 558 down until his death in 530 B.C., sees, for example, the conquest of Babylon, that fabled city of Mesopotamia. In that action, the Persians are transformed from outsiders and invaders to in one moment becoming the greatest imperial power of the ancient Near East. By the time of his death in 530 B.C., the Persian domain reached all the way from Afghanistan and the upper northwest of India all the way across central Asia as far as modern day Turkey, the Ionian Coast and the very edges of Greece. This was a vast and extraordinary empire.

As we look at the growth of Persian power, inevitably of course as the Persian Empire expanded, it brought them into contact with the Greeks. The Greeks of Asia Minor came under direct Persian control. Particularly after the conquest of Lydia, Persian control extended virtually all the way to the Aegean. You remember that ancient Greece included not only the Greek peninsula, but also the Ionian Coast, what we would nowadays call the coast of Turkey. By about 514 B.C., much of this was in Persian hands as well.

As this expansion was going on, of course the Greeks knew that there was a great power coming out of the East. They knew that there was a great power gobbling up the various smaller kingdoms and domains of Asia Minor. In the work of Herodotus, which we'll be examining more closely in the next lecture, we see the way in which the Greeks eventually would come to comprehend this and understand what was going on. In particular, if we look at the account of Croesus, the Lydian king who was eventually conquered by the Persians, what we find is that the Greeks were thinking of this in terms of what we might call not history, but rather a morality tale.

The expansion of the Persians was like an inexorable wave coming on. The reaction that it elicited from people as they came in contact with the Persians said much about them. For example, Croesus had believed that his power was invincible. He suffered, of course, for his arrogance. In retrospect, as the Greeks look back at the Persians and as they write stories to account for the growth of Persian power, they're thinking in terms of the lessons that are to be learnt there. They are lessons not just about who the Persians are, but what the Greeks have learnt from their contact with the Persians.

This Persian power which now, by the end of the sixth century B.C., is right on the very edges of the Greek world is an empire which by our standards we might call undergoverned. That is to say, there are no massive imperial bureaucracies. Rather, the Persians intelligently—in a stroke of genius in my opinion—recognized that the key to keeping their Empire together was to allow a certain amount of local autonomy. That local autonomy was not in the hands of the indigenous population. Rather, it was in the hands of the administrators given charge of these territories.

These territories of the Persian Empire were known as *satrapies*. We would call them "provinces." They often corresponded to the original territory of the various pre-Persian kingdoms. Rather than laying a heavy hand on their conquered territories, the Persians try to work with whatever style of government and whatever ethnic unit had existed before hand. In many cases, although a *satrap* (Persian governor) would be in place, in some instances even local rulers were allowed to retain their power, as long as they answered to a Persian-appointed overlord.

These *satraps* or governors that I've referred to enjoyed a great deal of independence. One of the reasons that the Persian king could afford to let them do this was that nearly all of them were his friends and relatives. We should think about this Empire in slightly different terms from the way we sometimes approach modern empires. We're looking really at the same kingdoms and the same ethnic groups as have existed for hundreds of years in the ancient Near East, but now with a new ruling elite drawn from the Persian royal family and its various lines.

Cyrus the Great died in 530 B.C. and he was succeeded by his son Cambyses. From the point of view of the Greeks, there was little during this period of the next eight years, from 530–522 B.C., that brought them into further contact with the Persians because Cambyses for much of that time was involved in putting down a rebellion in Egypt and reconquering it once again for the Persians.

He is remembered primarily from stories in Herodotus as a man who went mad by the end of his life and he raced around destroying sacred animals of the Egyptians. In fact, there's very little outside of these Greek sources to suggest that that's the truth about Cambyses. It's simply a lull in the expansion of the Persians into the domain of the Greek world.

After the death of Cambyses, there is a significant change in the affairs of the Persians. Again, the treatment of this by our Greek sources is quite revealing. In 522 B.C. after the death of Cambyses, Darius came to the throne. He was not the son of Cambyses, but rather from a collateral line of the Achaemenids. He came to the throne during a time when there was some dispute about whom the actual successor would be. After various negotiations and some conflict and murders within the royal household, Darius successfully established himself as the new king of the Persian Empire.

What is particularly interesting, though, is to turn away from the actual details of Darius' coming to the throne and to look once again at the way the Greeks thought about this and what they had to say. Herodotus in Book Three of his histories maintains that as the Persians were trying to determine who should succeed Cambyses, they held a constitutional debate.

In this constitutional debate, various Persian noblemen came forward and advocated changing the Persian system of government. One of these Persians maintained that the best system was in fact oligarchy, a system whereby only a narrow elite controls the kingdom. Then another came forward and said, no, in fact, democracy is better because that's the rule of the greatest number of people and that's the best system to have. Of course, finally one comes forward and says no, monarchy is really the best way to go and that's the view that triumphs. The Persians remain a monarchy.

If there are warning bells going in your head as you hear my recounting of Herodotus, then you're right. As one very good French scholar has said, "In this instance, the Persians are speaking Greek." I don't just mean that Herodotus, of course, has to write in Greek and so the speeches are recorded in Greek. The very conception that these people are playing with is a Greek conception about a choice of government: a monarchy, an oligarchy or a democracy. These are the choices that the Greeks of the fifth century B.C. were facing. They are not the choices that the Persians of the sixth century B.C. were facing.

What we find here is that at this level, the Greeks are betraying that they actually knew very little about the Persians at all if they seriously imagined that a group of Persian noblemen in the 520s B.C. could sit down and say, "Gee, you know maybe democracy would be a better route for the Persians." This is a fantasy—a concoction of the fifth century B.C. Greeks.

Darius continued not to worry about oligarchy or democracy, but rather to worry about what was really on the minds of the Persians and that was simply the matter of how to expand Persian power. He campaigned for the first time in Europe in Scythia. By about 514 B.C., under his expansion, Persian authority had reached right to the edge of the Aegean. Greek cities here had come under the control of the Persians, although in most places, the Persian *satraps* had been willing to put in a Greek tyrant to act as a kind of puppet governor.

The Persians, as I have pointed out, were generally content to leave native populations to rule themselves, provided the tribute was coming in to the Persian coffers. They did so here with the Greeks as well. Quite simply, Persian rule for the most part was not onerous, nor was it tyrannical. There were some exceptions, but for the most part it wasn't so. The best measure for this is quite simply that after Persian authority had been thrown off as a result of the Persian wars, the Athenians stepped in to create a league which required contributions from its various members. The contributions paid to the Athenians by their allies were assessed at the same amount as the tribute paid by the Greeks to their Persian overlords. I think that tells us something about the nature of Persian power. Perhaps it tells us more about the nature of Athenian power.

Nevertheless, all was not sweetness and light. In 499 B.C., there was a revolt of the Ionian Greek states against Persian authority, which culminated in the burning of Sardis by a Greek force, which included an Athenian contingent. This annoyed the great King of Persia immensely, as you can imagine. It set in train those momentous events which would lead to an invasion in 490 B.C. to punish the Athenians for the burning of Sardis, and then a second invasion in 480–479 B.C. where the entire Greek world would face the threat of coming under Persian control.

The details of that actual set of campaigns and the impact on the Greeks I'm going to deal with on another occasion. Again, I want to just finish off this part of the lecture by commenting on the way in which the Greeks thought about the Persians at this stage of their contact. Herodotus tells a story of one of the Persian kings in which he dreamt of seeing two beautiful women yoked together side-by-side. This dream was meant to suggest that one of the women was Europe and the other was Asia and that this dream was suggesting that Persian authority would eventually yoke together Europe and Asia—the Persians would conquer Europe as well.

What Herodotus' story tells us is that in the minds of the Greeks, there developed in the fifth century B.C. a very clear notion that the Persians were unlike them and that there was some deep and fundamental difference between the way the Persians did things and the way the Greeks did things. This even was located in geography. Asia and Europe were fundamentally different and the whole reason the Persians would eventually be defeated was that the gods would not tolerate one power uniting both Greece and Persia.

This notion of the Persian Wars as a massive cultural clash is something that took shape in the fifth century B.C. In the next lecture, I'm going to talk more about this and discuss the extraordinary significance of this, both for the Greeks and I think for the modern world as well. What I want to ask at this moment in the lecture is, "Is that what the Greeks and the Persians at the end of the sixth century B.C. really thought?" Not afterwards and not in hindsight, and not after the Greeks had won the war and decided that this enemy was a great enemy, but very unlike them. In the sixth century B.C., during the reign of Cyrus, Cambyses, and Darius, what actually was the contact between them? What was the difference between them? Were they really two completely antithetical systems?

I think the answer must be emphatically, no, they weren't. The Greeks were, in fact, divided among themselves into a number of different states. They were not a single Greek nation facing Persian might and power. They would only be that temporarily. The political choices that they made were not the same throughout Greece. Not every Greek state was a democracy facing the autocracy of Persia. Some were oligarchies. Some had kings. Some had tyrants. There was a great difference all across the Greek landscape. They were not the linear or the complete antithesis, if you will, of the Persians.

I think a much more important point to make is this: we see, thanks to the Greeks, a great clash between East and West, but in the context of the 490s B.C. and the world of around 500 B.C., the Greeks were insignificant in comparison to the Persians. They would become significant in terms of what their culture would leave for us and our connection to that culture, but I'm talking here about territory, power, empire and dominion. Seen in those terms, Greece is nothing more than the very last leg of a great journey that begins thousands of miles away in the Hindu Kush. Everything in between is Persian and only those last few inches on the map are Greek.

More importantly, not only is Greece relatively insignificant in terms of the whole expanse of the Persian Empire—this I think is really significant—there were many Greeks living and working in the Persian Empire. They did not think of the Persians as being a completely foreign and alien people who were the exact opposite of them. We know that, for example, as Persian power increased and as they called upon stonemasons to build their extraordinary palaces, they were importing Greeks from Ionia who were working quite happily in the Persian Empire. We know of Greeks who were actually living at the court of the great king, working for him: recording, acting as doctors for the great king, and so forth.

I think that it is a great mistake to think that at the time that the Greeks and the Persians first came into contact, there was an immediate sense that the two were destined to a final confrontation. That's a view that is dictated by subsequent events, but in fact at the time, I think the world must have looked very different indeed.

Enough of doing things from the Greek point of view. Let's see if just for a moment we can talk about the Persians themselves in their own terms. What do we know about this culture and this society that came in contact with the Greeks? The Achaemenid dynasty—the dynasty of Cyrus and his descendants—favored a traditional Persian religion, which was centered on the worship of natural elements and natural forces. Their gods appear to have been the sky, the moon, the sun, the earth, the fire, the water and so forth.

If, for example, you cross the Iranian plateau today, you will see often from miles in the distance these extraordinary fire altars where a sacred fire was kept burning in honor of the gods. They particularly honored—and here I'm talking not of the Persians in general, but of the ruling dynasty—the great sky god who they knew as Ahura-Mazda. If you see the great inscriptions at Bisitun, where the Achaemenid kings proclaimed their power using the same sort of language as Akkadian and Sumerian kings had used for millennia before them, the only difference is that the god who they show over them, quite literally as a winged figure above the figure of the king, will be this great sky god Ahura-Mazda. Here we see the Persians both adapting the customs of the earlier Near Eastern cultures and expressing something of their own particular identity and worship as well.

Because we've been so used to this idea of the Persians as being the opposite of the Greeks and as being a tyrannical empire ruled by despots, as soon as we talk about religion, we usually tend to think that this must have been an intolerant culture. In fact, our documentary evidence suggests exactly the opposite. In one extraordinary instance, we actually have a letter from Darius to one of his *satraps* who controlled an area that included Greek territory in which there was a sanctuary of Apollo. The letter from Darius says to his satrap, "Make sure that you do not cut down the trees of this god, for we have worshiped him long since, as did our ancestors."

In other words, in typical Near Eastern fashion, the tendency of the Persians was not to think of our gods as better than other gods, but to look for correspondences and ways that they could in fact worship other gods and bring their power to bear on the power of the Persian Empire itself.

The one area in which there really is a marked and undeniable difference between the Persians and the Greeks, and this would cause many great problems, was in the hierarchy of the Persian Empire. The Persian Empire assigned to each of its members a clear status, not only in terms of which ethnicity you had—whether you were Persian, Median, Sogdian or Bactrian—but also within the society of the court your level. The way that this was expressed was that if you met a superior, you were expected to prostrate yourself in an act the Greeks called *proskynesis*. You abase yourself physically. Then you are lifted by your superior who greets you. If you meet an equal, instead you greet that person with a kiss.

These gestures mark a very clear hierarchy. Of course, this would cause immense problems later when Greeks and Persians really had to live side-by-side under the reign of Alexander the Great. Once Alexander became the Persian king by ruling the Persian Empire, his Persian subjects wished to treat him as they would treat their king, with an act of obeisance and *proskynesis*. To a Greek, that was an action that you only performed in front of a god. Even in the realm of gesture, we can see a kind of fundamental divide. This one I won't deny, except that I will point out that the meanings of these gestures were different in the two cultures. To the Persians, the act meant showing honor to a superior. To the Greeks, it meant honoring a god. You see automatically there the room for misunderstanding between the two cultures even in something as simple as the meaning of a kiss.

We can say confidently that this was a military society. The Persians regarded themselves as a warrior aristocracy. Yet, even here, we also see something which will be fundamentally misinterpreted by the Greeks. Why? Because for the Persians, the signs of being members of this warrior aristocracy are that you are good at hunting and archery, and in particular are good at doing these things on horseback. You hunt on horseback and you fire your weapon. If you're very good, you may even be good enough to turn around and fire as you're fleeing from the enemy.

But to the Greeks, this is cowardly because to be a real fighter in the world of Greece 500 B.C. is of course to be a hoplite—to be a heavily armed infantryman. Even though really the codes and ideology of the two societies are very similar in honoring soldiers, the idea of what actually constitutes a soldier is very different in the two societies.

The Persian Empire, because it covered such a vast area, was able to call upon military contingents from many different areas. To the

Greeks, who were used to seeing one contingent of heavily armed hoplites fighting another contingent of heavily armed hoplites, the vision of the Persian army must have been absolutely astonishing. Rather than seeing the same thing repeated in every contingent, you would see lightly armed horsemen from the steppes. You would see Greek and Carian heavy infantrymen serving in the Persian army. You might see camel drivers from Africa. You might see people with lion skins or with tiger skins draped over them. You'd see light armed soldiers. You'd see people carrying wicker shields.

All these different forms of armament and all these different types of fighting all attested, in my mind, to the extraordinary power of the Persian Empire in uniting these different units, but was seen by the Greeks as a symbol of something else—of something foreign, peculiar and strange. There was nothing here that corresponded to what they saw as being the right way of fighting.

Of course the one thing that kept this Empire united was that it was all commanded by men who were called the "King's Friends." These were Persian officers.

If we turn aside from the aristocracy and from their fighting and from the military contingents, we find that if we look at the culture created by the Persians, what we have here is evidence for extremely refined culture. In the eyes of the Greeks, it was too refined. It was effete. It was feminine. The Greek version of this was helped by the fact that of course the Persians wore trousers. Trousers? Please. Greeks wear a chiton or a himation, a large garment that surrounds them completely. When they exercise, they do so heroically nude, not wearing trousers, which are something very suspect indeed from the point of view of the Greeks.

If we leave aside that Greek bias, what we have, in fact, is something very refined such as beautiful gold jewelry which reflects the nomadic origins of the Persians from the steppes. Here their Achaemenid art often takes over the motifs of earlier Near Eastern arts and reinterprets it even more brilliantly. They were a great culture.

The final aspect of Persian culture and life that I have to finish with is that of their monumental architecture. It is here in this architecture, and particularly in places such as Persepolis and the great hall, the Apadana, that we find the Persians expressing a monumental architecture that had not been a part of their earlier history, but which is something they have adopted from the ancient Near East. At these sites, even as they were built partly by Greek workmen and craftsmen working for them, the Persians produced something quite extraordinary and magnificent. These halls and palaces are bigger and more elaborate than anything they have ever produced and they are the lasting testament of the role and the rank of the Persians as the last of the great Near Eastern empires.

After their confrontation with the Greeks, they will eventually be conquered by the Greeks—by Alexander. At that moment, the Achaemenid dynasty will come to an end and Persian history, at least as we've known it up until this time, will follow a completely different trajectory.

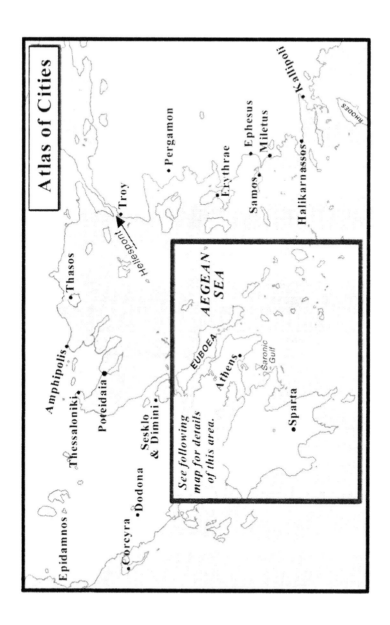

Atlas of Cities

AEGEAN SEA

See following map for details of this area.

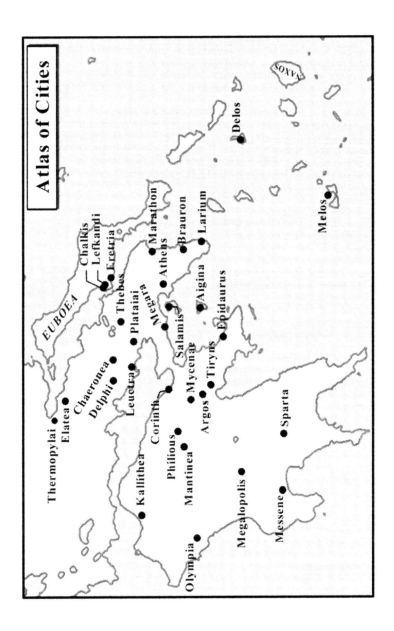

Atlas of Cities

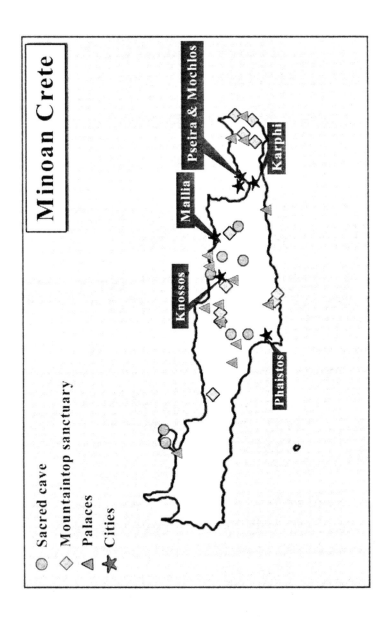

Minoan Crete

Sacred cave
Mountaintop sanctuary
Palaces
Cities

Psetra & Mochlos
Karphi
Mallia
Knossos
Phaistos

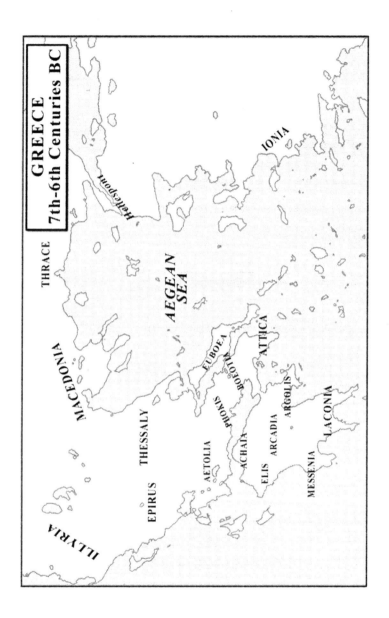

GREECE
7th-6th Centuries BC

THRACE

Hellespont

IONIA

AEGEAN SEA

MACEDONIA

EUBOEA

ATTICA

BOEOTIA

ARGOLIS

THESSALY

PHOKIS

ARCADIA

LACONIA

EPIRUS

AETOLIA

ACHAIA

ELIS

MESSENIA

ILLYRIA

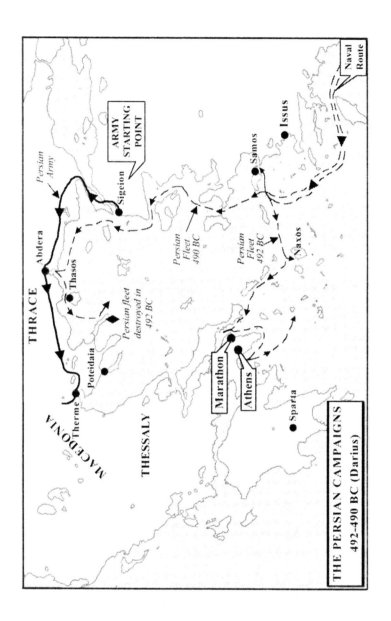

THE PERSIAN CAMPAIGNS
492–490 BC (Darius)

ARMY STARTING POINT

Persian Army

Persian Fleet 490 BC

Persian Fleet 492 BC

Persian fleet destroyed in 492 BC

Naval Route

THRACE

MACEDONIA

THESSALY

Abdera

Thasos

Poteidaia

Therme

Sigeion

Samos

Issus

Naxos

Marathon

Athens

Sparta

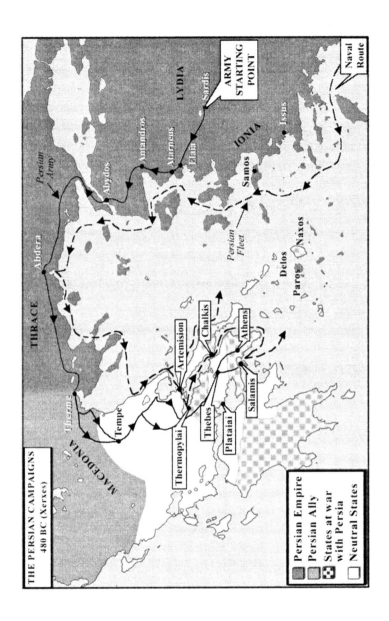

THE PERSIAN CAMPAIGNS
480 BC (Xerxes)

**Legend:**
- Persian Empire
- Persian Ally
- States at war with Persia
- Neutral States

**Labels on map:**
ARMY STARTING POINT
Naval Route
LYDIA
Sardis
IONIA
Issus
Samos
Naxos
Delos
Paros
Persian Army
Antandros
Atarneus
Elaia
Abydos
Persian Fleet
Abdera
THRACE
Chalkis
Athens
Artemision
Thermopylai
Thebes
Plataiai
Salamis
Therme
Tempe
MACEDONIA

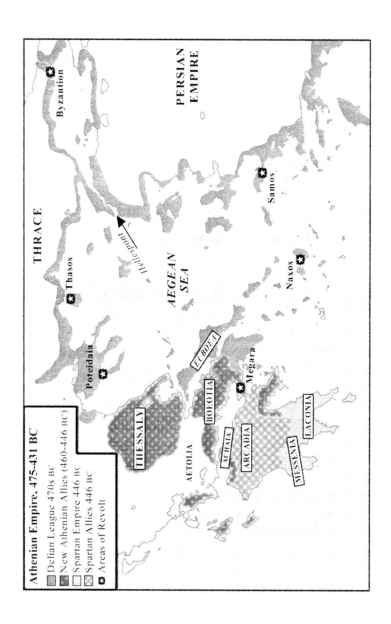

Athenian Empire, 475-431 BC

- Delian League 470s BC
- New Athenian Allies (460-446 BC)
- Spartan Empire 446 BC
- Spartan Allies 446 BC
- ✿ Areas of Revolt

THRACE

Byzantion

Thasos

Poteidaia

PERSIAN EMPIRE

Hellespont

AEGEAN SEA

Samos

Naxos

THESSALY

AETOLIA

EUBOEA

BOEOTIA

Megara

ACHAIA

ARCADIA

MESSENIA

LACONIA

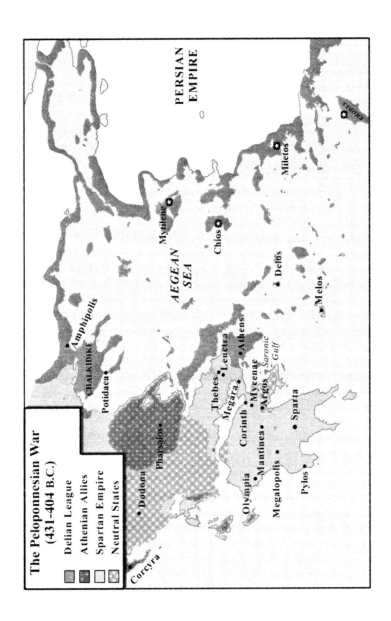

The Peloponnesian War
(431–404 B.C.)

Delian League
Athenian Allies
Spartan Empire
Neutral States

PERSIAN EMPIRE

AEGEAN SEA

Mytilene
Chios
Delos
Melos
Miletos

Amphipolis
CHALKIDIKE
Potidaea
Phasalos
Dodona
Corcyra

Thebes
Leuctra
Athens
Megara
Mycenae
Argos
Saronic Gulf
Corinth
Mantinea
Sparta
Olympia
Megalopolis
Pylos

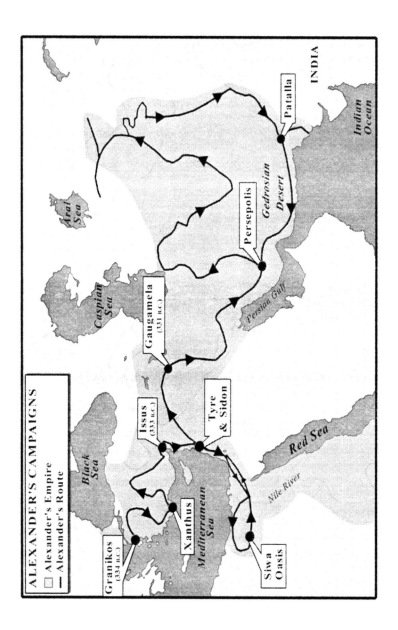

ALEXANDER'S CAMPAIGNS

☐ Alexander's Empire
— Alexander's Route

INDIA

Patalla

Indian Ocean

Aral Sea

Persepolis

Gedrosian Desert

Caspian Sea

Persian Gulf

Gaugamela
(331 B.C.)

Issus
(333 B.C.)

Tyre & Sidon

Red Sea

Black Sea

Xanthus

Mediterranean Sea

Nile River

Granikos
(334 B.C.)

Siwa Oasis

# Ancient Greek Civilization
# Timeline

c. 6000–2800 ..............................Neolithic Period

c. 2300–1900 ..............................Early Helladic Period (mainland)

c. 1900–1600 ..............................Middle Helladic Period (mainland)

c. 1900–1700 ..............................First Palatial Period (Crete)

c. 1700–1450 ..............................Second Palatial period (Crete)

c. 1600–1100 ..............................Late Helladic Period (mainland); Mycenaean civilization

c. 1450–1375 ..............................Mycenaean occupation of Cnossus

c. 1100–1000 ..............................Sub-Mycenaean Period.

c. 1000–900 .............................."Dark Ages," but signs of recovery at Lefkandi and Elateia

c. 900–700 ..............................Geometric Period

c. 800–700 ..............................Orientalizing Period

776 ............................................First Olympic Games

c. 750 ........................................Beginning of Greek colonization of Sicily, Italy, and the Black Sea

c. 725 ........................................Homer's poems written down

c. 700 ........................................Composition of Hesiod's poems

c. 650 ........................................Second Messenian War

594/3 ........................................Solon's archonship in Athens

561/0 ........................................Pisistratus' first attempt at tyranny

545–28/7 ....................................Pisistratus' tyranny at Athens

525 ............................................Cleisthenes' archonship

514 ............................................Assassination of Hipparchus, son of Pisistratus

510 ............................................Expulsion of Hippias, son of Pisistratus

508/7 ........................................Democratic reforms of Cleisthenes

490 ............................................Battle of Marathon

480 ............................................Battles of Thermopylae and Salamis

# Biographical Notes

**Alexander the Great:** Son of Philip II and remembered for the Greek conquest of the Persian Empire before his sudden death in 323 B.C.

**Aristotle:** Student of Plato and third of the great Greek philosophers, influential in a variety of areas, from ethics to biology.

**Cimon:** Leading politician in Athens in the generation after the Persian Wars.

**Cleisthenes:** Constitutional reformer whose innovations included the Council of 500, the ten tribes and system of demes and trittyes.

**Cleon:** the leading Athenian politician from c. 429–422 B.C.

**Cyrus the Great:** Persian king who ruled from 558–530 B.C., conquered the neighboring Medes and brought about the expansion of Persian power from Afghanistan to the Ionian coast.

**Darius I:** Persian king whose army was defeated at Marathon in 490 B.C.

**Darius III:** Persian king defeated by Alexander the Great. The last Achaemenid king of Persia.

**Dionysus**: God of Ecstasy, known to the Greeks as the One who Binds and Releases. Tragedy was performed in his honor.

**Evans, Sir Arthur:** British excavator of Cnossus and proponent of the view that Minoan Crete had colonized the mainland, giving rise to Mycenaean civilization.

**Hippias and Hipparchus:** Sons of Pisistratus. Hippias ruled from 528/7 to 510 B.C.

**Isagoras:** One of the leaders of the factional strife afflicting Athens from 510–508 B.C. Isagoras was supported by the Spartans, but defeated by his rival, Cleisthenes.

**Leonidas:** Spartan king at the time of the Persian invasions, he died at Thermopylae (480 B.C.).

**Lycurgus:** Legendary law-giver of Sparta.

**Menander:** Popular late 4th century playwright whose New Comedy blended romance, comedy and domestic situations.

**Nicias:** Unwilling and unlucky Athenian commander during the Sicilian Expedition (415–13 B.C.).

**Pisistratus:** Sixth century tyrant of Athens, responsible for unifying the Athenians and encouraging prosperity.

**Pericles:** Leading Athenian politician and general from c. 450–429 B.C.

**Philip II:** King of Macedon, 359–336 B.C., and responsible for the unification of Macedon, its expansion and the conquest of southern Greece.

**Plato:** Student of Socrates and perhaps the most influential of the Greek philosophers, especially associated with the theory of forms.

**Protagoras:** Best known of the sophists, he advocated a form of agnosticism.

**Schliemann, Heinrich:** German excavator whose work on Ithaca and at Troy and Mycenae constituted the first major excavations of the Aegean Bronze Age.

**Socrates:** Provocative Athenian philosopher who was executed in 399 B.C. on charges of impiety and corrupting the youth of Athens.

**Solon:** Athenian lawgiver responsible for wide-ranging political and economic reforms.

**Themistocles:** Athenian leader at the time of the Persian invasions, he was remembered for convincing the Greeks to stay and fight at Salamis.

**Xenophon:** Athenian gentleman, soldier, and writer whose literary works included history, biography, and political pamphlets, as well as instruction manuals on cavalry tactics, hunting and household management.

**Xerxes:** Persian king whose invasion of Greece in 480–79 B.C. was defeated at Salamis and Plataea.

# Bibliography

Andrewes, A. (1956) *The Greek Tyrants*. London: Hutchinson.

Bicknell, P.J. (1972) "Kleisthenes as Politician: An Exploration," in *Studies in Athenian Politics and Genealogy* (= *Historia Einzelschriften* Heft 19).

Burkert, W. (1985) *Greek Religion: Archaic and Classical*. Oxford: Oxford University Press.

Cartledge, P. (1979) *Sparta and Lakonia: a Regional History 1300-362 B.C.* London: Routledge.

_____ (1993) *The Greeks. A Portrait of Self and Others*. Oxford: Opus Books.

Davies, J.K. (1982) *Democracy and Classical Athens*. Cambridge, Mass.: Harvard University Press.

Desborough, V.R. d'A. (1964) *The Last Mycenaeans and their Successors, an Archaeological Survey, c. 1200-c.1000 B.C.* Oxford: Clarendon Press.

_____ (1972) *The Greek Dark Ages*. New York: St Martin's Press.

Dougherty, C. (1993) *The Poetics of Colonization. From City to Text in Archaic Greece*. Oxford: Oxford University Press.

Eliot, C.W.J. (1962) *Coastal Demes of Attika: A Study of the Policy of Kleisthenes*. Toronto: University of Toronto Press.

Finley, M.I. (1980) *Ancient Slavery and Modern Ideology*. London: Chatto and Windus.

_____ (1981) *Economy and Society in Ancient Greece*. London: Chatto and Windus.

Graham, A.J. (1964) *Colony and Mother City in Ancient Greece*. New York: Barnes & Noble.

Green, P. (1990) *Alexander to Actium*. Berkeley: University of California Press.

Hartog, F. (1988) *The Mirror of Herodotus. The Representation of the Other in the Writing of History*. Berkeley: University of California Press.

Hignett, C. (1952) *A History of the Athenian Constitution*. Oxford: Oxford University Press.

Hurwit, J.M. (1985)*The Art and Culture of early Greece, 1100-480 B.C.* Ithaca: Cornell University Press.

Kagan, D.W. (1969) *The Outbreak of the Peloponnesian War*. Ithaca: Cornell University Press.

Malkin, (1987) *Religion and Colonization in Ancient Greece*. Leiden: Brill.

Marchand, S.L. (1996) *Down from Olympus. Archaeology and Philhellenism in Germany, 1750-1970*. Princeton: Princeton University Press.

Marinatos, N. (1984) *Art and Religion in Thera*. Athens: Ekdotike Athenon.

Meiggs, R. (1972) *The Athenian Empire*. Oxford: Oxford University Press.

Morgan, C. (1990) *Athletes and Oracles. The Transformation of Olympia and Delphi in the eighth century B.C.* Cambridge: Cambridge University Press.

Neils, J. ed. (1992) *Goddess and Polis: The Panathenaic Festival in Ancient Athens*. Princeton: Princeton University Press.

Pouncey, P.R. (1980) *The Necessities of War: A Study of Thucydidean Pessimism*. New York: Columbia University Press.

Rolley, C., Jacquemin, A. and Laroche, D., eds (1990) *Delphes. Oracles, Cultes et Jeux*. Les Dossiers d'Archéologie 151 Dijon.

Romilly, J. de (1992) *The Great Sophists in Periclean Athens*. Oxford: Oxford University Press.

Sealey, R. (1976) *A History of the Greek City States*. Berkeley: University of California Press.

Snodgrass, A.M. (1971) *The Dark Age of Greece*. Edinburgh: The University Press.

Ste Croix, G.E.M. de (1972) *The Origins of the Peloponneian War*. Ithaca: Cornell University Press.

Traill, D.A. (1993) *Excavating Schliemann*. Illinois Classical Studies, Supplement 4. Atlanta: Scholar's Press.

Warren, P. (1989) *The Aegean Civilizations*. New York: Peter Bedrick Books.

Winkler, J.J. (1990) *The Constraints of Desire: the Anthropology of Sex and Gender in Ancient Greece.* New York: Routledge.

Wood, M. (1985) *In Search of the Trojan War*. New York: Facts On File.

Zeitlin, F. and Winkler, J., eds (1990) *Nothing to Do with Dionysos?* Princeton: Princeton University Press.